SIXTEEN
COUNSELING SESSIONS
WITH THE
WONDERFUL
COUNSELOR

God's personal counsel to individuals

as recorded in the Bible

BY DAN PETERS

Designed for small groups, adult Sunday School Classes
and your own personal study

(Includes leaders' guide)

xulon
PRESS

TABLE OF CONTENTS:

Introduction

AN APPOINTMENT WITH THE "WONDERFUL COUNSELOR"

I was upset! The young divorced mom we were trying to help was in trouble! She had irrational fears. On one occasion, she thought bugs were crawling all over her so she tried to tear her clothes off. Another time, she thought that some of her clothes were from the Devil. She started throwing her clothes away. She got in such a fearful state that her loving relatives encouraged her to commit herself to a private mental hospital where we visited her for several months. They said she was psychotic. She was now medicated but still fearful and hallucinating. She didn't seem better, just slower. I was so concerned that I called a Christian counselor and set up an appointment for her. We had her sign herself out and drove her directly to the Christian counselor's office. She was in that room for a long time. When she came out, she was at peace. The problem that had been at the root of her symptoms was resolved. She came to our home, where we were caring for her young children. She lived with us for several months. She got a job and an apartment. She eventually married a fine Christian man and has been living for the Lord with no more psychotic episodes.

That Christian counseling session was over 35 years ago. What did that Christian counselor say to her in that 90 minute session that made all the difference in her life? I wanted to find out! I began to study with that counselor and others. What began with my questions has led to a lifelong study of Christian counseling. Christian counseling deals with sin, forgiveness and the power of the Holy Spirit to change us. I learned a lot from several Christian counselors who applied the Bible to counseling.

Then, after many years of counseling, God led me into a deeper understanding. It began with a study of

Isaiah 9:6 where the Messiah is predicted to be the "Wonderful Counselor". (There is no comma in the original Hebrew). I began thinking about how God Himself counseled individuals as recorded in the Bible. I looked at how God counseled Cain, Hagar, Job, Gideon, Miriam, David, Jonah, Elijah, Isaiah, Daniel, the woman at the well, the rich young ruler, the woman caught in adultery, Peter and Paul.

I began to see a pattern of technique that God Himself used to help these individuals with problems like, anger, abuse, grief, racism, lust, guilt, inferiority, exhaustion, bitterness, shame, emptiness, materialism, adultery, skepticism, depression and affliction. I noticed how God, the Wonderful Counselor, asked questions, gave encouragement, gave options, warned of consequences and predicted outcomes. I learned much about God, myself and counseling. What a study it has been! I am so excited about it that I am now sharing what I have learned with you. As you read this book, I am praying that God will use it to not only glorify Himself but that He will also use it to help those who seek to follow the example of the "Wonderful Counselor".

This book is designed for small groups, teen and adult Sunday School classes, and personal study. By completing one chapter each week this book will be finished in four months. Or use it for a monthly Men's Breakfast meeting. It can be used for Bible College classroom reading or for individual study for pastors or Christian counselors.

You can lecture the basics of the Bible passage, ask discussion questions, share your insights and pray together. Answers to the discussion questions are in the Leaders' Guide at the end of the book. These lessons were originally prepared for a missions training seminar with Crossworld Mission in Banas, Ecuador.

There are no references to the Hebrew or Greek text of the Scriptures. I have studied these passages in the original languages but decided to limit this book to insights that can be gained by a reading of the texts in the New King James version, which is provided for your study. You may want to underline or highlight as you study and make notes in the margin.

DEDICATION

This book is dedicated to the Lord Jesus Christ, who is the Wonderful Counselor, and to my wonderful wife, Diane, who has often spoken wonderful counsel into my life when I most needed it.

ACKNOWLEDGEMENTS

The Elders of Limerick Chapel so willingly gave me the gift of time to write this book. They are Dave Brunner, Bob Uhler, Randy Egolf, Gary Rapp and Mike Kuntz. The one-month sabbatical was a wonderful way to encourage me to start writing after 43 years of pastoral work and 25 years as Senior Pastor of Limerick Chapel. The people of the Chapel have been such a blessing to me as they seek the counsel of the Wonderful Counselor. Dave and Ida May Brunner have sponsored this book. Pastor Kendall Harris assumed my pastoral duties for a month. Pastors Dale Gregory and Bob Spare have encouraged me for which I am grateful. Dr. Walter Croom carefully edited the whole book and suggested ideas and words for the chapter on Elijah. Pastor Dale Gregory, Jim Hepner, Pastor Rick Leineweber, Dr. Doug Finkbiener, Larry and

Linda Depue, Bill Harding and Pastor Dave Jones have reviewed and made helpful suggestions for this book. To God be the glory!

Explanation of case studies at the beginning of each chapter: These are based on true stories. They have been modified to remove any reference that could be a negative reflection on anyone living or dead. The stories relating to my sins and failures are true.

ENDORSEMENTS

"Having taught biblical counseling for over 30 years through the Institute of Christian Counseling and at home and abroad, I can heartily recommend the book "Sixteen Sessions with the WONDERFUL COUNSELOR" by Dr. Daniel Peters. Here you will find practical, straight-from the shoulder help for people in need with loving, sensitive concern. God's Word is skillfully woven into the material lending the note of God's authority. "Sixteen Sessions with the WONDERFUL COUNSELOR" is a good book to give to counselees and a great book in helping to train lay people.

Walt Croom, Ph.D

General Director

Military Evangelism, Inc.

"The longer I am in ministry, the more obvious it is to me that sin has crushed and ruined so many lives and that direct biblical counsel is needed more than ever before, both from the pulpit and person-to-person. In "Sixteen Sessions with the WONDERFUL COUNSELOR" Dan Peters wastes no words as he mines from the wealth of Scripture the wisdom and ways of our God in applying His truth to a variety of real-life situations. Great value is found in the stimulating questions at the end of each chapter and then even greater value is discovered in his wise answers in the back of the book. This is a concise and sharp tool in equipping one another to aid others in their battle with sin and its difficult effects."

David A. Jones–Pastor of Campbell Memorial Baptist Church in WV.

"The book, "Sixteen Sessions with the WONDERFUL COUNSELOR," will be a useful training tool for existing and new volunteer Client Advisors in our ministry. Each week we counsel young ladies that have often experienced abuse, anger, grief, shame, guilt, emptiness, and depression because of sexual immorality and possibly a past abortion. Sin always has consequences, and our focus is to take young ladies to God's Word to better understand their sin-addicted state and how they can turn away from it. From there we help them to see what Jesus has done for them and how they might have eternal life. Through this book, we can successfully counsel ladies using Scriptures to help them understand the issues they face as well as God's response to it. The counsel given in Scripture helps clients to see they are not alone in their sins, and the thought-provoking questions will help them apply Biblical truths to their situation (2 Timothy 3:16-17). In addition, this book will also be a valuable tool for my staff and myself in our personal lives and in our churches as we reach out to others outside the ministry."

Dianne Pomon R.N., Executive Director of Genesis Pregnancy Care Center, Pottstown, Pa and author of "The Disappearance of Shame" published by Southwest Radio Church.

"This book isn't another self-help book based upon pop psychology. Dan Peters has gleaned some wonderful insights from the Bible on how God himself counseled people. Dan observes that the "Wonderful Counselor" asked questions, gave encouragement, gave options, warned of consequences and predicted outcomes. These alone are worth the price of the book. This is a wonderful tool to get to know God better and how to counsel others in these same areas. As an Expositor of the Bible and a biblical counselor that I've respected over the years, Dan consistently allows the text of Scripture to speak for itself rather than reading into it. This is one of the highest compliments that I could give anyone. Every Christian is to be competent to counsel one another in these areas. This book is a wonderful tool to train future pastors. This is a must read for pastors, counselors and small group members."

Rick Leineweber, Pastor of Small Groups at Atlantic Shores Baptist Church and Head Consultant for BiblicalDisciplemaking.NET

"I read your book and think it is fantastic. Your simple Bible-based approach to life's most tangled issues is both inspiring and refreshing in an age that promotes the wisdom of man. You have reinforced to me once again that there is no substitute for our relationship with the LORD in leading others out of the wilderness of despair. There can be no doubt when such a one is rescued by your counsel that it is the Wonderful Counselor who gets the credit. One verse came to my mind after I read this that described the disciples after the resurrection in Acts where the people took note that the disciples had "been with Jesus", not how smart they were or that they had all the answers now."

Dr. David Nelson, President, Founder
& Executive Director at Crossing Cultures
International.

"It has been a blessing to be under the teaching of Pastor Peters. One of the outstanding features of his teaching is his God-given ability to clearly teach and apply the Word. In "Sixteen Sessions with the WONDERFUL COUNSELOR", he uses this gift in writing to give us a book that will be a blessing to many."

Larry Depue, veteran missionary with New Tribes Mission in Bolivia, South America.

"There is no better example for us to follow than the real life practices and illustrations of the Son of God when He walked on this earth and the examples of men of God who gave Godly counsel to those around them, and that is what you have given us in your book. I also appreciate your personal illustrations and willingness to open your own heart and life to your readers."

Tom Kweder, missionary to Indonesia and President of Worldwide Tentmakers, Inc.

Chapter One

CAIN – ANGER

"That woman makes me so angry!" Why was Rob so angry at his wife? Why do we get so angry sometimes? What does anger do to us? How does it blind us to the consequences of our actions? How can we bring it under God's control so we don't hurt others or ourselves?

The Problem:

Cain was so angry that he killed his brother, Abel. How did he become so angry? And how did God Himself counsel Cain in his anger?

Genesis 4:1–15 Now Adam knew Eve his wife, and she conceived and bore Cain, and said, "I have acquired a man from the Lord." ² Then she bore again, this time his brother Abel. Now Abel was a keeper of sheep, but Cain was a tiller of the ground. ³ And in the process of time it came to pass that Cain brought an offering of the fruit of the ground to the Lord. ⁴ Abel also brought of the firstborn of his flock and of their fat. And the Lord respected Abel and his offering, ⁵ but He did not respect Cain and his offering. And Cain was very angry, and his countenance fell.

⁶ So the Lord said to Cain, "Why are you angry? And why has your countenance fallen? ⁷ If you do well, will you not be accepted? And if you do not do well, sin lies at the door. And its desire is for you, but you should rule over it."

⁸ Now Cain talked with Abel his brother; and it came to pass, when they were in the field, that Cain rose up against Abel his brother and killed him.

⁹ Then the Lord said to Cain, "Where is Abel your brother?"

He said, "I do not know. Am I my brother's keeper?"

[10] And He said, "What have you done? The voice of your brother's blood cries out to Me from the ground. [11] So now you are cursed from the earth, which has opened its mouth to receive your brother's blood from your hand. [12] When you till the ground, it shall no longer yield its strength to you. A fugitive and a vagabond you shall be on the earth."

[13] And Cain said to the Lord, "My punishment is greater than I can bear! [14] Surely You have driven me out this day from the face of the ground; I shall be hidden from Your face; I shall be a fugitive and a vagabond on the earth, and it will happen that anyone who finds me will kill me."

[15] And the Lord said to him, "Therefore, whoever kills Cain, vengeance shall be taken on him sevenfold." And the Lord set a mark on Cain, lest anyone finding him should kill him.

Cain's offering was not respected by the Lord. Hebrews 11:4 tells us that Abel's offering was accepted because it was brought in faith. When Cain realized that God had accepted Abel's offering and not his own, he became angry. His face fell. He looked mad and sad. The New Testament commentary on this passage is found in 1 John 3:11-12: *"For this is the message that you heard from the beginning, that we should love one another, [12] not as Cain who was of the wicked one and murdered his brother. And why did he murder him? Because his works were evil and his brother's righteous."* Cain's anger led to murder. But between those two events, God personally counseled Cain:

The Counsel:

How did God Himself counsel Cain? First God asked him two "why" questions: "Why are you angry?" and "Why has your countenance fallen?" Then God gave Cain two options and told him what the outcome of each was: *"If you do well, will you not be accepted? And if you do not do well, sin lies at the door"*. Acceptance was what Cain wanted. The Lord showed him how to obtain it. Just "do well". The New Testament gives this counsel in Ephesians 4:26–27: *"Be angry, and do not sin": do not let the sun go down on your wrath, 27 nor give place to the devil."*

The alternative offered was, "do not do well". The consequence of that choice was laid out: "sin lies at the door". Then God gives some insight to help Cain make a good choice: "And its desire is for you, but you should rule over it". Sin crouches like a lion at Cain's door, but he should rule over that sin. Satan goes around like a roaring lion seeking whom he may devour (1 Peter 5:8). The Devil wants to steal from you, kill you and destroy you (John 10:10). But God is greater! (1 John 4:4)

The Response:

Even with counsel from the Wonderful Counselor, Cain did not do well. He let sinful anger eat him up. It desired to consume him and he did not rule over it. Proverbs 16:32 says, *"He who is slow to anger is better than the mighty, and he who rules his spirit than he who takes a city".* Cain went out from the counseling session he had with God Himself and demonstrated his willful disregard for everything God had said. He let his rejection become anger. Then his anger turned to depression. His depression resulted in violence. He then talked with his brother Abel, rose up against him and killed him. This was the first murder in human history. It must have surprised Cain that his brother did not recover. No one had ever physically died before Abel.

And the Lord did not give up dealing with Cain: "Then the Lord said to Cain, "Where is Abel your brother?" He said, "I do not know. Am I my brother's keeper?" Why did God ask Cain where his brother was? Did God want information? No, God wanted Cain to think about the whereabouts of his brother. Where was Abel? His body lay in the field, perhaps hidden under something. His soul was in Heaven since his blood sacrifice was accepted. But Abel's blood had a voice: "The voice of your brother's blood cries out to me from the ground" (Genesis 3:10). All through the Bible, blood is presented as having a voice that God hears. Hebrews 12:24: *"to Jesus the Mediator of the new covenant, and to the blood of sprinkling that speaks better things than that of Abel."* Abel's blood cried out to God for justice. Jesus' blood cries out to the Father for mercy on those who have trusted in Jesus. It is on the basis of His blood that Jesus ever lives to intercede for us (Hebrews 7:25). God had another question: "What have you done?"

The Consequences:

God announces a curse on Cain: "So now you are cursed from the earth, which has opened its mouth to receive your brother's blood from your hand. When you till the ground, it shall no longer yield its strength to you. A fugitive and a vagabond you shall be on the earth." Cain then complains about the curse: "My punishment is more than I can bear

… whoever finds me will kill me". We see that God is considerate even when we fail. God responds in grace to Cain's complaint about his sentence: "Therefore, whoever kills Cain, vengeance shall be taken on him seven-fold." God then put a mark on Cain, lest anyone finding him should kill him. God protected Cain with a marking that let people know that God would avenge his death seven times.

Discussion Questions:

1. Why did God respect Abel's offering but not Cain's?

2. How do you think Cain's face looked when his countenance fell while he was very angry?

3. Is there a link between anger and depression?

4. Is there a link between depression and violence?

5. Why do you think God asked Cain so many questions?

6. Why did God give Cain two options? Why not just tell him what to do?

7. What insight did the Lord share with Cain? How would you use this phrase in counseling someone?

8. What do you think Cain said to Abel before he killed him?

9. How might this story have turned out differently?

10. What good did God's counsel do for Cain?

11. What have you learned about God from this study?

12. What did you learn about counseling from this study?

13. What did you learn about yourself from this study?

Chapter Two:

HAGAR – ABUSE

Holly's brother began sexually molesting her when she was six. Now she is thirteen and her brother is in jail. She hates her mother for not protecting her. Her father has left the family for another woman. She comes to you for help. What do you tell her?

The Problem:

Hagar started her life as an Egyptian slave. Then she was bought in a slave market by a couple with a strange religion (the man claimed God had spoken to him). They took her far from her home into Canaan. Her master was a sometimes dishonest man named Abram. He made her a slave wife (concubine) to him when his free wife, Sarai, couldn't conceive a baby. When Hagar conceived, Sarai got jealous and threw her out of the house. In the desert, she met God and He gave her perfect counsel:

Genesis 16:1–16 Now Sarai, Abram's wife, had borne him no children. And she had an Egyptian maidservant whose name was Hagar. ² So Sarai said to Abram, "See now, the Lord has restrained me from bearing children. Please, go in to my maid; perhaps I shall obtain children by her." And Abram heeded the voice of Sarai. ³ Then Sarai, Abram's wife, took Hagar her maid, the Egyptian, and gave her to her husband Abram to be his wife, after Abram had dwelt ten years in the land of Canaan. ⁴ So he went in to Hagar, and she conceived. And when she saw that she had conceived, her mistress became despised in her eyes.

⁵ Then Sarai said to Abram, "My wrong be upon you! I gave my maid into your embrace; and when she saw that she had conceived, I became despised in her eyes. The Lord judge between you and me."

⁶ So Abram said to Sarai, "Indeed your maid is in your hand; do to her as you please." And when Sarai dealt harshly with her, she fled from her presence.

⁷ Now the Angel of the Lord found her by a spring of water in the wilderness, by the spring on the way to Shur. ⁸ And He said, "Hagar, Sarai's maid, where have you come from, and where are you going?"

She said, "I am fleeing from the presence of my mistress Sarai."

⁹ The Angel of the Lord said to her, "Return to your mistress, and submit yourself under her hand." ¹⁰ Then the Angel of the Lord said to her, "I will multiply your descendants exceedingly, so that they shall not be counted for multitude." ¹¹ And the Angel of the Lord said to her:

"Behold, you are with child,
And you shall bear a son.

<u>You shall call his name Ishmael,</u>
<u>Because the Lord has heard your affliction.</u>
<u>12 He shall be a wild man;</u>
<u>His hand shall be against every man,</u>
<u>And every man's hand against him.</u>
<u>And he shall dwell in the presence of all his</u>
<u>brethren."</u>

13 Then she called the name of the Lord who spoke to her, You-Are- the-God-Who-Sees; for she said, "Have I also here seen Him who sees me?" 14 Therefore the well was called Beer Lahai Roi; observe, it is between Kadesh and Bered.

15 So Hagar bore Abram a son; and Abram named his son, whom Hagar bore, Ishmael. 16 Abram was eighty-six years old when Hagar bore Ishmael to Abram.

So, there was a childless wife (Sarai), an impatient husband (Abram) and a pregnant runaway servant wife (Hagar), all in the same (dysfunctional) family. Hagar was proud. She despised Sarai who was in charge of her in the family. She had a bad attitude towards authority, and no wonder! Sarai was bossy and Abram was passive and evasive.

Sarai dealt harshly with Hagar, so Hagar fled her home. But that is not the end of the story. In the desert, by a spring of water on the road to Shur, she met the Lord. How did the Wonderful Counselor counsel her?

The Counsel:

The Wonderful Counselor reinforced her authority structure by addressing her as: "Hagar, Sarai's maid" and then He asked her two questions: "where have you come from?" and "where are you going?"

If you can adequately answer these two questions, you will begin to understand yourself and who you are. The Lord knew where she came from and He knew where she was headed. He wanted her to think about it. When she answered His question, He gave her very direct counsel: "Return to your mistress Sarai and submit yourself under her hand." Wow! That is very direct! "Return and submit".

Do you have the courage to tell people to return to those imperfect people under whose authority they are and do what they say? Sometimes the solution to a tricky situation is to consider the authority structure under which God has placed that person.

Now if a parent or spouse has assaulted a person, they should be arrested and dealt with by the law of the land.

But Christians who counsel should not encourage people to rebel against God-given authorities. In 1 Peter 3, we see how a wife can win her husband to obedience towards God: 1 Peter 3:1–6, *"__Wives, likewise, be submissive to your own husbands, that even if some do not obey the word, they, without a word, may be won by the conduct of their wives,__ ² when they observe your chaste conduct accompanied by fear. ³ Do not let your adornment be merely outward—arranging the hair, wearing gold, or putting on fine apparel— ⁴ rather let it be the hidden person of the heart, with the incorruptible* *beauty of a gentle and quiet spirit, which is very precious in the sight of God. ⁵ For in this manner, in former times, the holy women who trusted in God also adorned themselves, being submissive to their own husbands, ⁶ <u>as Sarah obeyed Abraham, calling him lord, whose daughters you are if you do good and are not afraid with any terror.</u>"*

Before the story of her life was over, Sarah learned to submit obediently to her passive and sometimes dishonest husband, Abraham. She is given as an example of submission in the New Testament, but it did not come naturally to her. She learned it in the laboratory of real life in a dysfunctional home.

In Genesis 16:11, we see that the Lord listened to Hagar: "The Lord has heard your affliction". So we see that the Wonderful Counselor asks good questions and He listens well. He looked carefully at her according to verse 13: "Then she called the name of the Lord who spoke to her, You Are The God Who Sees; for she said, 'Have I also here seen Him who sees me?'" Non-verbal signs reveal much to a good counselor.

He encouraged her with a wonderful promise in verse 10: ***"Then the Angel of the Lord said to her, 'I will multiply your descendants exceedingly, so that they shall not be counted for multitude.'"***

The Lord revealed to Hagar that her son would be a wild man (vs. 12). Hagar was being counseled to expect trouble with her son. Here we see that the Wonderful Counselor knows that some children are more difficult to raise than others, even though Ishmael's father was the father of faith and was greatly blessed.

The Lord helped her to see her answer when she had trouble noticing solutions to her problems. In Genesis 21:19, "Then God opened her eyes, and she saw a well of water. And she went and filled the skin with water, and gave the lad a drink." A good counselor helps the person himself discover solutions to his or her problems. Proverbs 20:5 says, ***"Counsel in the heart of man is like deep water, but a man of understanding will draw it out."*** Asking probing questions can help people to face themselves and think as the Prodigal did in Luke

15:17-18: "And when he came to himself he said … I will arise and go to my father, and say to him, "Father, I have sinned against heaven and before you,". In Acts 12:11 *And when Peter had come to himself, he said, "Now I know for certain that the Lord has sent His angel, and has delivered me from the hand of Herod,".* Bringing others to a place where they see themselves in honest evaluation of their true relationship with God is one of the goals of Christian counseling.

The Response:

Hagar's response is amazing! What an excellent counselee! She names the Lord, "You are the One Who Sees". She realizes that she has seen the Lord. She names the well: "The well of the One who lives and sees me". She goes beyond solving her immediate problem and comes to know the Lord on a much deeper level than before she had her problem. The ultimate goal of Christian counseling is that our counselees would get to know God better.

41

Then they can go to Him directly and eliminate the middle man (the human counselor).

The most amazing result of this counsel is that Hagar did "return and submit". That takes a lot of humility and grace. And she had it. But it is the key to the blessing of God on her life and the life of her son, Ishmael. Hagar becomes the mother of a great nation. All of the great Arab people groups are derived from this abused Egyptian slave wife who responded beautifully to the Wonderful Counselor. In Genesis 20:20, we read, ***"So God was with the lad; and he grew and dwelt in the wilderness, and became an archer."***

Will we see Hagar and Ishmael in Heaven?

Discussion Questions:

1. How would you have counseled Sarai when she seemed to be infertile?

2. How would you have conducted marriage counseling with Abram and Sarai in this conflict over Hagar despising Sarai?

3. Is there ever a time to send an abused wife back to an abusive situation?

4. Why do you think the Lord asked Hagar where she had come from?

5. Why do you think the Lord asked Hagar where she was going?

6. What did Hagar learn about God?

7. According to Genesis 21:17, what was Hagar's problem?

8. How can we help people open their eyes to see God's solutions?

9. What have you learned about God from this study?

10. What have you learned about counseling from this study?

11. What have you learned about yourself from this study?

Chapter Three:

Job–Grief

O ur son, Nathan, was seven years old when God took him home to Heaven. He was riding his bike with his brothers. A bus ran over him and instantly killed him. One of the most difficult things I ever did was to tell my precious wife, Diane, that our Nathan was dead. How do we deal with grief? According to the Bible, God Himself counseled a man named Job. He lost everything except God, his nagging wife and his critical "friends".

The Problem:

Job 1:13–2:1 "Now there was a day when his sons and daughters were eating and drinking wine in their oldest brother's house; ¹⁴ and a messenger came to Job and said, "The oxen were plowing and the donkeys feeding beside them, ¹⁵ when the

Sabeans raided them and took them away—indeed they have killed the servants with the edge of the sword; and I alone have escaped to tell you!"

[16] While he was still speaking, another also came and said, "The fire of God fell from heaven and burned up the sheep and the servants, and consumed them; and I alone have escaped to tell you!"

[17] While he was still speaking, another also came and said, "The Chaldeans formed three bands, raided the camels and took them away, yes, and killed the servants with the edge of the sword; and I alone have escaped to tell you!"

[18] While he was still speaking, another also came and said, "Your sons and daughters were eating and drinking wine in their oldest brother's house, [19] and suddenly a great wind came from across the wilderness and struck the four corners of the house, and it fell on the young people, and they are dead; and I alone have escaped to tell you!"

²⁰ Then Job arose, tore his robe, and shaved his head; and he fell to the ground and worshiped. ²¹ And he said:

"Naked I came from my mother's womb,
And naked shall I return there.
The Lord gave, and the Lord has taken away;
Blessed be the name of the Lord."
²² In all this Job did not sin nor charge God with wrong."

Before this story is over, Job has lost his wealth, his children and his health. His wife discourages him. His friends criticize him. Job gets depressed and wants to die (Job chapter 3).

The Counsel:

When Job's friends have finished blaming Job himself for all his troubles, God shows up in chapter 38 and asks some good questions:

"Then the Lord answered Job out of the whirl-wind, and said:

[2] "Who is this who darkens counsel
By words without knowledge?
[3] Now prepare yourself like a man;
I will question you, and you shall answer Me.
[4] "Where were you when I laid the foundations of the earth?
Tell Me, if you have understanding."

These questions were asked to make Job think about who he was and who God is. Good Christian counseling moves people out of their problem-focus to a God-focus. When they see who God is, they can begin to start thinking about what they lost and what it all means.

God points out to Job that He has made the heavens and the earth and all of the animals and plants. In Job 38 God takes Job to the "science center (verses 8-30) the "planetarium" (verses 31-33) and to the "zoo" (39-41). Sometimes what a grieving persons needs is to get out of the house and take a walk in a beautiful natural setting. Waterfalls, mountains and ocean views do something healthy for us. They show us how small we are and how great God is.

Job's answer to God's questions demonstrates that he gets the point. In Job 40:3-5 we read, "Then Job answered the Lord and said:

⁴ "Behold, I am vile;
What shall I answer You?
I lay my hand over my mouth.
⁵ Once I have spoken, but I will not answer;
Yes, twice, but I will proceed no further."

Job now has a new view of God and of himself. We read in Job 42:1-6:

"Then Job answered the Lord and said:
² "I know that You can do everything,
And that no purpose of Yours can be with-held from You.
³ You asked, 'Who is this who hides counsel without knowledge?'

Therefore I have uttered what I did not understand,
Things too wonderful for me, which I did not know.
⁴ Listen, please, and let me speak;
You said, 'I will question you, and you shall answer Me.'
⁵ "I have heard of You by the hearing of the ear,
But now my eye sees You.
⁶ Therefore I abhor myself,
And repent in dust and ashes."

Job has a new view of God and thus a new view of himself.

The Consequences:

Job 42:7–17 And so it was, after the Lord had spoken these words to Job, that the Lord said to Eliphaz the Temanite, "My wrath is aroused against you and your two friends, for you have not spoken of Me what is right, as My servant Job has. ⁸ Now therefore, take for yourselves seven bulls and seven rams, go to My servant Job, and offer up for yourselves a burnt offering; and My servant Job shall pray for you. For I will accept him, lest I deal with you according to your folly; because you have not spoken of Me what is right, as My servant Job has."

⁹ So Eliphaz the Temanite and Bildad the Shuhite and Zophar the Naamathite went and did as the Lord commanded them; for the Lord had accepted Job. ¹⁰ And the Lord restored Job's losses when he prayed for his friends. Indeed the Lord gave Job twice as much as he had before. ¹¹ Then all his brothers, all his sisters, and all those who had been his acquaintances before, came to him and ate food with him in his house; and they consoled him and comforted him for all the adversity that the Lord had brought upon him. Each one gave him a piece of silver and each a ring of gold.

¹² Now the Lord blessed the latter days of Job more than his beginning; for he had fourteen thousand sheep, six thousand camels, one thousand yoke of oxen, and one thousand female donkeys. **¹³ He also had seven sons and three daughters. ¹⁴ And he called the name of the first Jemimah, the name of the second Keziah, and the name of the third Keren-Happuch. ¹⁵ In all the land were found no women so beautiful as the daughters of Job; and their father gave them an inheritance among their brothers.**

¹⁶ After this Job lived one hundred and forty years, and saw his children and grandchildren for four generations. ¹⁷ So Job died, old and full of days.

The Lord corrected Job's critical friends. The Lord commended Job. The Lord reconciled his friends to Himself and to Job through prayer and sacrifice. The Lord restored Job's losses when he prayed for his friends. Job's friends ate with him and brought him gifts. They consoled and comforted him. The Lord restored Job's family. The Lord blessed Job more than at the beginning with wealth and health.

Discussion Questions:

1. Why did God allow Satan to do such terrible things to Job?

2. What are some ways that Satan can attack Christians?

3. Are losses always the result of sins in our lives?

4. Why did God ask Job so many questions?

5. Why did God take Job to the "Zoo" and "Planetarium"?

6. How can we know what God is doing with people so we don't give wrong counsel like Job's counselors did?

7. How important is reconciliation in dealing with grief?

8. How can we help people to be reconciled to loved ones when they are grieving?

9. What have we learned from Job about God?

10. What have we learned about God from Job?

11. What have we learned about ourselves from Job?

Chapter Four:

GIDEON – INFERIORITY

66 **I** 'm no good! I can't do anything right! I should just give up trying to please my mother! She is such a perfectionist! I quit!" Patty decided that she might as well drop out of college. She wasn't making good grades anyway. It seemed like such a waste of money. She has come to you for counsel. What will you say?

The Problem:

Judges 6:1–6 Then the children of Israel did evil in the sight of the Lord. So the Lord delivered them into the hand of Midian for seven years, [2] and the hand of Midian prevailed against Israel. Because of the Midianites, the children of Israel made for themselves the dens, the caves, and the strongholds which are in the mountains. ³ So it was, whenever Israel had sown, Midianites would come up; also Amalekites and the people of the East would come up against them. ⁴ Then they would encamp against them and destroy the produce of the earth as far as Gaza, and leave no sustenance for Israel, neither sheep nor ox nor donkey. ⁵ For they would come up with their livestock and their tents, coming in as numerous as locusts; both they and their camels were without number; and they would enter the land to destroy it. ⁶ So Israel was greatly impoverished because of the Midianites, and the children of Israel cried out to the Lord.

God was judging Israel because they had begun worshipping the gods of the Amorites (Judges 6:10). Gideon was the man chosen by God to deliver Israel when they cried out to the Lord for help:

Judges 6:11–12 Now the Angel of the Lord came and sat under the terebinth tree which was in

Ophrah, which belonged to Joash the Abiezrite, while his son Gideon threshed wheat in the winepress, in order to hide it from the Midianites. [12] And the Angel of the Lord appeared to him, and said to him, "The Lord is with you, you mighty man of valor!"

But Gideon didn't think that the Lord was with him: *Judges 6:13 Gideon said to Him, "O my lord, if the Lord is with us, why then has all this happened to us? And where are all His miracles which our fathers told us about, saying, 'Did not the Lord bring us up from Egypt?' But now the Lord has forsaken us and delivered us into the hands of the Midianites."*

The Counsel:

The Lord tells Gideon that he is a "mighty man of valor" (verse 12). Then God tells him to "Go in this might of yours." (verse 14) Then God promises Gideon deliverance of the nation: "you shall save Israel from the hand of the Midianites".

God reminds Gideon that He has sent him: "Have not I sent you?" Gideon still has objections to this task; *"O my Lord, how can I save Israel? Indeed my clan is the weakest in Manassah, and I am the least in my father's house."* (Judges 6:15) The Lord's counsel to Gideon was, "Surely I will be with you, and you shall defeat the Midianites as one man." Gideon wants a sign. God gives him a sign of fire that destroys the sacrifice (verse 21).

The Outcome:

God told Gideon to begin by destroying his father's idol of Baal and substituting an offering to the Lord. Gideon obeys. His success leads Gideon to the big confrontation with the Midianites. Gideon "puts out the fleece" twice and God graciously gives him the signs he desires. Gideon is now ready to obey God and wins a great victory.

Discussion Questions:

1. Why do you think that the Lord chose Gideon to deliver Israel?

2. How could the Lord say that Gideon was a "mighty man of valor" when Gideon hadn't won any battles?

3. What does it mean "the Lord is with you"?

4. Why had God forsaken Israel to their enemies for a time?

5. Why does God choose to work through people who have human weaknesses?

6. Why did Gideon need so many signs?

7. Why did God give Gideon so many signs?

8. Why did the Lord give Gideon a small task before sending him into the big battle?

9. What have you learned from this study about God?

10. What have you learned from this study about counseling?

11. What have you learned from this study about yourself?

Chapter Five:

MIRIAM – RACISM

O ur "white" daughter wanted to marry a man from Haiti that she had met at a Christian college. We found a lot of reasons to be against it. Some of them were pretty good reasons, but one of them was a bad reason. I didn't want her to marry a "black" man. Since then I have learned to respect this new son-in-law. He is a good worker, a fine husband and a wonderful father. I love him like a son. But it didn't start out that way.

The Problem:

Miriam didn't like her brother's choice of a wife. She was an Ethiopian. So she criticized him. She cloaked her racism in an attack on the unique position of Moses before God and the nation of Israel. Racism is often cloaked in other criticisms.

Numbers 12:1–3 "Then Miriam and Aaron spoke against Moses because of the Ethiopian woman whom he had married; for he had married an Ethiopian woman. ² So they said, "Has the Lord indeed spoken only through Moses? Has He not spoken through us also?" And the Lord heard it. ³ (Now the man Moses was very humble, more than all men who were on the face of the earth.)

Miriam and Aaron spoke against Moses because he had married an Ethiopian woman. Notice that they didn't speak to Moses. They spoke to other people about him. They probably asked their friends, "What do you think about Moses' new wife?" When Jesus taught about the Church that would be founded on Himself, He only established one rule Himself. He left the rest to be revealed through Paul and others. What did Jesus consider so important that He taught it Himself rather than wait until the Apostles could do it?

Matthew 18:15–17, <u>"Moreover if your brother sins</u>
<u>against you, go and tell him his fault between you</u>
<u>and him alone. If he hears you, you have gained</u>
<u>your brother.</u> [16] But if he will not hear, take with
you one or two more, that 'by the mouth of two or
three witnesses every word may be established.' [17]
And if he refuses to hear them, tell it to the church.
But if he refuses even to hear the church, let him
be to you like a heathen and a tax collector."

Jesus wanted his followers to talk to each other and resolve problems themselves on a personal level. He forbade them from talking about each other without addressing themselves to the one with whem they were upset. Gossip and backbiting have destroyed many a church and family. The clearest evidence of a dysfunctional home is that people talk about each other but do not talk to each other about their problems.

1 Peter 4:15, "But let none of you suffer as a murderer, a thief, an evildoer, or as a busybody in other people's matters."

The Counsel:

Numbers 12:4-9 <u>Suddenly the Lord said to Moses, Aaron, and Miriam, "Come out, you three, to the tabernacle of meeting!" So the three came out. ⁵ Then the Lord came down in the pillar of cloud and stood in the door of the tabernacle, and called Aaron and Miriam. And they both went forward. ⁶ Then He said, "Hear now My words: If there is a prophet among you, I, the Lord, make Myself known to him in a vision; I speak to him in a dream. ⁷ Not so with My servant Moses; He is faithful in all My house. ⁸ I speak with him face to face, Even plainly, and not in dark sayings; And he sees the form of the Lord. Why then were you not afraid To speak against My servant Moses?" ⁹ So the anger of the Lord was aroused against them, and He departed.</u>

God Himself called Moses, Aaron and Miriam to the tabernacle of meeting. "Come out, you three, to the tabernacle of meeting!" God says. Then God came down in the pillar of cloud and stood in the door of the tabernacle and called Aaron and Miriam. And they both went forward. He told them that Moses was faithful. He told them that unlike the other prophets, He spoke to Moses face to face. Then the Lord asked Aaron and Miriam a thought-provoking question: "Why were you not afraid to speak against My servant Moses?"

God was angry and He departed, leaving them to think about what He just said. The next thing that happened was that Miriam became leprous, white as snow. So we see the Lord backed up His counsel with discipline.

The Wonderful Counselor said he would back up the discipline of those of us who counsel according to His Word (Matthew 18:18–20), ***"Assuredly, I say to you, <u>whatever you bind on earth will be bound in heaven, and whatever you loose on</u>***

earth will be loosed in heaven. ¹⁹ Again I say to you that if two of you agree on earth concerning anything that they ask, it will be done for them by My Father in heaven. ²⁰ For where two or three are gathered together in My name, I am there in the midst of them."

In 1 Corinthians 11:27–32 we read, *"Therefore whoever eats this bread or drinks this cup of the Lord in an unworthy manner will be guilty of the body and blood of the Lord. ²⁸ But let a man examine himself, and so let him eat of the bread and drink of the cup. ²⁹ For he who eats and drinks in an unworthy manner eats and drinks judgment to himself, not discerning the Lord's body. ³⁰ For this reason many are weak and sick among you, and many sleep. ³¹ For if we would judge ourselves, we would not be judged. ³² But when we are judged, we are chastened by the Lord, that we may not be condemned with the world."*

A person who rebels against the discipline of the church and takes communion while under church discipline will be disciplined by God with weakness, sickness or premature death. One of the marks of true Biblical counseling is that it is done in the context of a local church. Local church authority backs up the counsel given in private with witnesses and church discipline leading to excommunication. I have seen this process produce repentance and forsaking of sin and a sweet willingness to correct the wrongs and be restored to fellowship. One married couple who were going to get a divorce due to the husband's adultery repented when confronted with the necessity of the counselor to back up the counsel with church discipline. Sadly many churches fail to practice church discipline especially in cases involving divorce.

The Outcome:

Numbers 12:10-15 *And when the cloud departed from above the tabernacle, suddenly Miriam became leprous, as white as snow. Then Aaron turned toward Miriam, and there she was, a leper.* *[11] So Aaron said to Moses, "Oh, my lord! Please do not lay this sin on us, in which we have done* *foolishly and in which we have sinned. ¹² Please do not let her be as one dead, whose flesh is half consumed when he comes out of his mother's womb!"*

¹³ So Moses cried out to the Lord, saying, "Please heal her, O God, I pray!"

¹⁴ <u>Then the Lord said to Moses, "If her father had but spit in her face, would she not be shamed seven days? Let her be shut out of the camp seven days, and afterward she may be received again." </u> ¹⁵ So Miriam was shut out of the camp seven days, and the people did not journey till Miriam was brought in again."

Miriam's sudden onset of leprosy after the sudden, angry departure of the Lord led to Aaron speaking very respectfully to his brother, Moses. "Oh, my lord! Please do not lay this sin on us in which we have done foolishly and in which we have sinned." Aaron made a humble confession of sin. That response is always a miracle of God's grace when it happens in a counseling session. They had begun by gossiping behind Moses' back and now they are humbly admitting that they have sinned. When a criticism session turns into a counseling session, it is God's work. Aaron then intercedes for his sister, Miriam. "Please do not let her be as one dead, whose flesh is half consumed when he comes out of his mother's womb!" Moses, who, according to verse two, is more humble than all men who were on the face of the earth, prays to the Lord for Miriam. "Please heal her, O God, I pray!" The Lord agreed with Moses' prayer but ordered that Miriam be given a "time out" for seven days and then let back into the camp again. Apparently the Lord thought Miriam needed a week to work on her attitude before returning to fellowship with God's people again.

Discussion Questions:

1. Do you believe that marriage between different ethnic groups is morally wrong? Why or why not?

2. How would you counsel a couple who wanted to marry across ethnic groups?

3. Why is gossip so damaging to families and churches?

4. How do you avoid gossip?

5. How do you guard the confidentiality of the counseling session?

6. How should we respond to someone who begins sharing negative information about a Christian leader?

7. How should we counsel family members who are not speaking to each other?

8. Under what circumstances should we move from counseling into church discipline?

9. Can racism hinder the work of the gospel in evangelism and missions today?

10. What have you learned about God from this event?

11. What have you learned about counseling from this account?

12. What have you learned about yourself from this study?

The Counsel:

Second Samuel 12:1–12 Then the Lord sent Nathan to David. And he came to him, and said to him: "There were two men in one city, one rich and the other poor. ² The rich man had exceedingly many flocks and herds. ³ But the poor man had nothing, except one little ewe lamb which he had bought and nourished; and it grew up together with him and with his children. It ate of his own food and drank from his own cup and lay in his bosom; and it was like a daughter to him. ⁴ And a traveler came to the rich man, who refused to take from his own flock and from his own herd to prepare one for the wayfaring man who had come to him; but he took the poor man's lamb and prepared it for the man who had come to him."

⁵ So David's anger was greatly aroused against the man, and he said to Nathan, "As the Lord lives, the man who has done this shall surely die! ⁶ And he shall restore fourfold for the lamb, because he did this thing and because he had no pity."

⁷ Then Nathan said to David, "You are the man! <u>*Thus says the Lord God of Israel: 'I anointed you king over Israel, and I delivered you from the hand of Saul. ⁸ I gave you your master's house and your master's wives into your keeping, and gave you the house of Israel and Judah. And if that had been too little, I also would have given you much more! ⁹ Why have you despised the commandment of the Lord, to do evil in His sight? You have killed Uriah the Hittite with the sword; you have taken his wife to be your wife, and have killed him with the sword of the people of Ammon. ¹⁰ Now therefore, the sword shall never depart from your house, because you have despised Me, and have taken the wife of Uriah the Hittite to be your wife.' ¹¹ Thus says the Lord: 'Behold, I will raise up adversity against you from your own house; and I will take your wives before your eyes and give them to your neighbor, and he shall lie*</u>

*__with your wives in the sight of this sun. 12 For you
did it secretly, but I will do this thing before all
Israel, before the sun.'__*"

The Lord sent Nathan the prophet to David.
Nathan told David a story about a rich man who
had many sheep, but who stole the one little lamb
owned by a poor man. David reacted violently.
From his kingly throne he pronounced a death
sentence and four-fold restitution for the case. He
said, "As the Lord lives, the man who has done this
shall surely die!" Nathan then turned the tables by
saying, "You are the man."

David over-reacted because guilty people have
great difficulty seeing other people's sins correctly.
That is why Jesus said that we should take the "beam"
out of our own eye so we can see clearly to remove
the speck from our brother's eye (Matthew 7:3-5).
A Christian counselor who has a guilty conscience
is unfit to help others. Paul the Apostle testified that
he exercised himself to have a conscience empty of
guilt before God and man (Acts 24:16). Confessing

our faults to God and those we have wronged will make us wise counselors of others. If you do not have to confess anything to God or others regularly, you are unfit to be a Christian counselor (1 John 1:6-10 and James 5:16).

The Wonderful Counselor then tells David that he is ungrateful. He tells him that he is a thief. He tells him that he is a murderer. Then he pronounces the Lord's sentence on David's crimes: The sword will never depart from his house. God will raise up adversity against David from his own house. God will publicly give his wives to another. David's sins were secret, but his humiliation and shame will be public.

The Outcome:

2 Samuel 12:13-15 *So David said to Nathan, "I have sinned against the Lord."*

And Nathan said to David, "The Lord also has put away your sin; you shall not die. ¹⁴ However, because by this deed you have given great occasion to the enemies of the Lord to blaspheme, the child also who is born to you shall surely die." [15] Then Nathan departed to his house."

David confessed his sins to his merciful Heavenly Father and asked Him for cleansing and restoration. Psalm 51 is the prayer he prayed on this occasion:

Psalm 51 To the Chief Musician. A Psalm of David When Nathan the Prophet Went to Him, After He Had Gone in to Bathsheba.
[1] Have mercy upon me, O God,
According to Your lovingkindness;
According to the multitude of Your tender mercies,
Blot out my transgressions.
[2] Wash me thoroughly from my iniquity,
And cleanse me from my sin.
[3] For I acknowledge my transgressions,
And my sin is always before me.
[4] Against You, You only, have I sinned,
And done this evil in Your sight—

That You may be found just when You speak,

And blameless when You judge.

⁵ *Behold, I was brought forth in iniquity,*

And in sin my mother conceived me.

⁶ *Behold, You desire truth in the inward parts,*

And in the hidden part You will make me to know wisdom.

⁷ *Purge me with hyssop, and I shall be clean;*

Wash me, and I shall be whiter than snow.

⁸ *Make me hear joy and gladness,*

That the bones You have broken may rejoice.

⁹ *Hide Your face from my sins,*

And blot out all my iniquities.

¹⁰ *Create in me a clean heart, O God,*

And renew a steadfast spirit within me.

¹¹ *Do not cast me away from Your presence,*

And do not take Your Holy Spirit from me.

¹² *Restore to me the joy of Your salvation,*

And uphold me by Your generous Spirit.

¹³ *Then I will teach transgressors Your ways,*

And sinners shall be converted to You.

¹⁴ *Deliver me from the guilt of bloodshed, O God,*

The God of my salvation,

And my tongue shall sing aloud of Your righteousness.

15 O Lord, open my lips,

And my mouth shall show forth Your praise.

16 For You do not desire sacrifice, or else I would give it;

You do not delight in burnt offering.

17 The sacrifices of God are a broken spirit,

A broken and a contrite heart—

These, O God, You will not despise.

18 Do good in Your good pleasure to Zion;

Build the walls of Jerusalem.

19 Then You shall be pleased with the sacrifices of righteousness,

With burnt offering and whole burnt offering;

Then they shall offer bulls on Your altar.

This prayer of confession would be a good one to use with anyone who needs to know how to get right with God.

Nathan told David that the Lord had forgiven him. "The Lord has put away (forgiven) your sin. You shall not die." But because David's sin had given great occasion to the enemies of the Lord to blaspheme, there would be grave consequences. Nathan said, "The child also who is born to you shall surely die." The child did die and God showed His grace by choosing Bathsheba's later son, Solomon, to be the next and great King of Israel.

Discussion Questions:

1. Why do men have such a problem with pornography?

2. How would you counsel a man who is addicted to pornography?

3. How would you counsel a man who didn't work because he didn't need the money?

4. Why did Nathan need to start his counseling with a story?

5. What does an outburst of anger tell you about a counselee?

6. What does a lack of gratefulness have to do with immorality?

7. What is the connection between immoral Christian leaders and the progress of evangelism and missions?

8. What have you learned about God in this study?

9. What have you learned about counseling in this study?

10. What have you learned about yourself in this study?

Chapter Seven:

ELIJAH – EXHAUSTION

Pastor Smith had had it. After being away overseas for a week of special meetings in which so many people had been saved, he was sick and tired. This morning the wife of the Chairman of the Church Board has called and criticized him for not visiting her mother-in-law. She told him that if he didn't stop being away so much, she was going to see to it that he would be fired and she would see to it that no church in their denomination would ever hire him. Pastor Smith wanted to die. He just couldn't face another day back at his home church. He comes to you for counsel. What will you tell him?

The Problem:

1 Kings 19:1–4And Ahab told Jezebel all that Elijah had done, also how he had executed all the prophets with the sword. ² Then Jezebel sent a messenger to Elijah, saying, "So let the gods do to me, and more also, if I do not make your life as the life of one of them by tomorrow about this time." ³ And when he saw that, he arose and ran for his life, and went to Beersheba, which belongs to Judah, and left his servant there.

⁴ But he himself went a day's journey into the wilderness, and came and sat down under a broom tree. And he prayed that he might die, and said, "It is enough! Now, Lord, take my life, for I am no better than my fathers!"

Elijah has just experienced the greatest victory of his life and ministry. But he is tired and depleted. Even Jesus was depleted by ministry: Luke 6:19 says "power went out from him". Luke 8:46

says, "I perceived that power went out from me". Whenever we minister to others, power goes out of us. In order to continue to minister, power must go back into us. Some of the greatest failures came after the greatest victories. Think of Noah getting drunk and naked after the ark landed. Think of King David sinning with Bathsheba after defeating so many enemies. Think of Solomon bowing to idols after being used of God to write Scripture and build a temple for God. "Let him who thinks he stands take heed lest he fall." (1 Corinthians 10:12).

Jezebel had threatened him with death. He ran away and abandoned his servant. He just wanted to be alone. He went into the wilderness and sat down under a tree and prayed for death. He wanted to end it all.

The Counsel:

1 Kings 19:5–18 Then as he lay and slept under a broom tree, suddenly an angel touched him, and said to him, "Arise and eat." ⁶ Then he looked, and there by his head was a cake baked on coals, and a jar of water. So he ate and drank, and lay down again. ⁷ And the angel of the Lord came back the second time, and touched him, and said, "Arise and eat, because the journey is too great for you." ⁸ So he arose, and ate and drank; and he went in the strength of that food forty days and forty nights as far as Horeb, the mountain of God.

⁹ And there he went into a cave, and spent the night in that place; and behold, the word of the Lord came to him, and He said to him, "What are you doing here, Elijah?"

¹⁰ So he said, "I have been very zealous for the Lord God of hosts; for the children of Israel have forsaken Your covenant, torn down Your altars, and killed Your prophets with the sword. I alone am left; and they seek to take my life."

¹¹ Then He said, "Go out, and stand on the mountain before the Lord." And behold, the Lord passed by, and a great and strong wind tore into the mountains and broke the rocks in pieces before the Lord, but the Lord was not in the wind; and after the wind an earthquake, but the Lord was not in the earthquake; ¹² and after the earthquake a fire, but the Lord was not in the fire; and after the fire a still small voice.

¹³ So it was, when Elijah heard it, that he wrapped his face in his mantle and went out and stood in the entrance of the cave. Suddenly a voice came to him, and said, "What are you doing here, Elijah?"

¹⁴ And he said, "I have been very zealous for the Lord God of hosts; because the children of Israel have forsaken Your covenant, torn down Your altars, and killed Your prophets with the sword. I alone am left; and they seek to take my life."

¹⁵ Then the Lord said to him: "Go, return on your way to the Wilderness of Damascus; and when you arrive, anoint Hazael as king over Syria. ¹⁶

Also you shall anoint Jehu the son of Nimshi as king over Israel. And Elisha the son of Shaphat of Abel Meholah you shall anoint as prophet in your place. [17] It shall be that whoever escapes the sword of Hazael, Jehu will kill; and whoever escapes the sword of Jehu, Elisha will kill. [18] Yet I have reserved seven thousand in Israel, all whose knees have not bowed to Baal, and every mouth that has not kissed him."

God separates Elijah for a time from the rest of the world for the purpose of ministering to him. (Sometimes taking a month off or taking a vacation can be helpful. Sometimes we can't see the forest for the trees.) God ministers to Elijah by providing food and rest. (Sometimes changing a person's diet can be very helpful.) After Elijah is in a proper frame of mind and well rested, God takes him deeper into the wilderness and communicates to him through an object lesson. God is obviously making the point that He is greater than fire, wind and even an earthquake. Yes, He is even greater than Jezebel. He doesn't have to worry or be afraid or feel intimidated because the greatest force in the universe has His back. And furthermore He doesn't always communicate through fire, wind and earthquakes. Sometimes He communicates in a small, still voice. Perhaps He is telling Elijah that He doesn't have to be bringing down fire from heaven which is a very exhausting thing to do. Perhaps there is a message here for pastors. Pastors don't have to be setting Sunday school records or always being in a building program. Big is not always better. Big does not necessarily mean success. Elijah was successful on Mount Carmel, but the day after he was on the run.

God not only uses separation, food and rest, and an object lesson but He also uses the technique of asking questions, "Elijah, what are you doing here?" And when Elijah says that isn't so, God gently reminds him that he has his facts wrong. God reminds him that He has seven thousand that have not bowed their knees to Baal.

The Outcome:

As the counseling session winds down, God gives Elijah a new assignment, a homework assignment, if you will. God's counseling method obviously worked because Elijah obeyed his Lord and followed through on his assignment.

Discussion Questions:

1. Why did the Lord let Elijah sleep and then give him cake and water before the counseling session began? (verses 5-7).

2. Why did the Lord ask Elijah "What are you doing here?" (verse 9).

3. Why did Elijah think that he was the only one doing God's will and caring about the Lord's work? (verse 10).

4. Why did the Lord ask Elijah again, "What are you doing here?" (verse 13).

5. Why did the Lord give him several tasks to do?

6. Are you the only one who is seeking to serve the Lord in your situation?

7. What have you learned about God from this study?

8. What have you learned about counseling from this study?

9. What have you learned about yourself from this study?

Chapter Eight:

JONAH – BITTERNESS

Joe and Mary were missionaries. They had successfully planted several churches in nearby towns in their own country. But now the Lord was leading them to move to a nation that had terrorized their people and invaded their beloved nation. But Joe and Mary knew this couldn't really be what God wanted. They knew that these people were no good. They were convinced that they were arrogant and vicious. They deserved judgment from God, not the good news of the gospel. Joe and Mary decided that they would go somewhere more productive. Those people didn't deserve missionaries.

__The Problem:__

Jonah has finally gone and done what God wanted him to do. He has preached to the people he hated. God has done what Jonah knew He would do. God has forgiven the Ninevites and has decided not to destroy them. Job was angry with the Ninevites, but now he is angry with God:

Jonah 4:1–3 But it displeased Jonah exceedingly, and he became angry. ² So he prayed to the Lord, and said, "Ah, Lord, was not this what I said when I was still in my country? Therefore I fled previously to Tarshish; for I know that You are a gracious and merciful God, slow to anger and abundant in lovingkindness, One who relents from doing harm. ³ Therefore now, O Lord, please take my life from me, for it is better for me to die than to live!"

Jonah is so bitter at God that he asks God to kill him. He would rather die than live like this.

Bitterness is a root that springs up and defiles many (Hebrews 12:15). Bitterness results from letting the sun go down on our wrath and giving the Devil a place in our lives (Ephesians 4:26-27).

The Counsel:

Jonah 4:4–11 Then the Lord said, "Is it right for you to be angry?"

⁵ So Jonah went out of the city and sat on the east side of the city. There he made himself a shelter and sat under it in the shade, till he might see what would become of the city. ⁶ And the Lord God prepared a plant and made it come up over Jonah, that it might be shade for his head to deliver him from his misery. So Jonah was very grateful for the plant. ⁷ But as morning dawned the next day God prepared a worm, and it so damaged the plant that it withered. ⁸ And it happened, when the sun arose, that God prepared a vehement east wind; and the sun beat on Jonah's head, so that he grew faint. Then he wished death for himself, and said, "It is better for me to die than to live."

⁹ Then God said to Jonah, "Is it right for you to be angry about the plant?"

And he said, "It is right for me to be angry, even to death!"

¹⁰ But the Lord said, "You have had pity on the plant for which you have not labored, nor made it grow, which came up in a night and perished in a night. ¹¹ And should I not pity Nineveh, that great city, in which are more than one hundred and twenty thousand persons who cannot discern between their right hand and their left—and much livestock?

The Lord begins with a probing question: "Is it right for you to be angry?" (verse 4). "Is it right?" is a good question to ask any person who is bitter. Bitterness is a sin that is obvious to everyone but the one who is bitter, because bitterness is all about other people and their wrongs. Asking a bitter person to consider the morality of their own anger is a good place to start. Many wives are bitter about their husband's infidelity or lack of care. They relive the events that have caused them hurt and are able to relive and rehearse the hurts over and over again.

Next, Jonah is angry about the shade plant that God had provided and then removed. Again Jonah wants to die. God again asks, "Is it right for you to be angry..? about the plant? Jonah answers in verse 9: "It is right for me to be angry, even to death!". The plant was an object lesson. God wanted Jonah to have as much pity for Nineveh as Jonah had for the plant. God made the Ninevites. He had pity on them because he saw them ruining themselves as well as the Israelites. He cares for the people who don't know their right hand from their left and he cares about the animals. Those who can't tell their right hand from their left would include the children, the mentally handicapped and perhaps others.

God cares for people and so should we. Why do some people care more for animals than they do for people? Perhaps it is because animals have generally treated them better than people who have deeply hurt them.

The Outcome:

Jonah ends the story without repenting of his bitterness.

Discussion Questions:

1. Did Jonah know God well?

2. How bitter was Jonah?

3. Did Jonah answer God's question the first time God asked it?

4. How did God get Jonah to answer His question?

5. What was God's final question to Jonah?

6. What have you learned from this study about God?

7. What have you learned from this study about counseling?

8. What have you learned from this study about yourself?

Chapter Nine

ISAIAH – GUILT

J ack has a filthy mouth. He sprinkles his sentences with four letter-words and appears to be unaware of it. But one Sunday he is sitting in church with his family. He hears about how great God is and listens to the choir sing, "Holy, Holy, Holy". He listens as a children choir sings, "the whole earth is full of God's glory". He thinks about himself and decides that his life is a mess. He doesn't belong here. He has a dirty mouth, and the people he works with every day talk worse than he does. He wants to change so he meets the pastor at the door after church and makes an appointment to meet for counseling. How should the pastor start?

The Problem:

Isaiah 6:1–13 In the year that King Uzziah died, I saw the Lord sitting on a throne, high and lifted up, and the train of His robe filled the temple. ² Above it stood seraphim; each one had six wings: with two he covered his face, with two he covered his feet, and with two he flew. ³ And one cried to another and said:

"Holy, holy, holy is the Lord of hosts;
The whole earth is full of His glory!"
⁴ And the posts of the door were shaken by the voice of him who cried out, and the house was filled with smoke.
⁵ So I said:
"Woe is me, for I am undone!
Because I am a man of unclean lips,
And I dwell in the midst of a people of unclean lips;
For my eyes have seen the King,
The Lord of hosts."

King Uzziah has died. The throne is empty. God revealed Himself to Isaiah in such a way that Isaiah saw the Lord. The angels cried, "Holy, holy, holy… the whole earth is full of His glory!" But Isaiah is full of woe. He is undone. He has unclean lips and he dwells with people who have unclean lips. He has a dirty mouth. Job had a similar experience. In Job 42:5–6 we read: "I have heard of You by the hearing of the ear, but now my eye sees You. ⁶ Therefore I abhor myself, and repent in dust and ashes."

The first step in a personal revival is to be thoroughly disgusted with yourself. If your worship experience doesn't show you how sinful you are by comparison with our Holy God, you are missing something.

The Counsel:

Isaiah 6:6-8a: *Then one of the seraphim flew to me, having in his hand a live coal which he had taken with the tongs from the altar. ⁷ And he touched my mouth with it, and said: "Behold, this has touched your lips;*

Your iniquity is taken away,
And your sin purged."
⁸ Also I heard the voice of the Lord, saying:
"Whom shall I send,
And who will go for Us?"

God sent an angel with a live coal from the altar. When it touched Isaiah's lips, his sin was cleansed. The angel said, "Your iniquity is taken away, and your sin is purged." Once Isaiah had confessed his sin and been forgiven, the Lord had work for him to do. God called him to be a messenger.

We cannot serve God until our relationship and fellowship with God is restored through a process of adoration, confession and yieldedness.

The Outcome:

Isaiah 6:8b-13 Then I said, "Here am I! Send me."
9 And He said, "Go, and tell this people:
'Keep on hearing, but do not understand;
Keep on seeing, but do not perceive.'

[10] *"Make the heart of this people dull,*

And their ears heavy,

And shut their eyes;

Lest they see with their eyes,

And hear with their ears,

And understand with their heart,

And return and be healed."

[11] *Then I said, "Lord, how long?"*

And He answered:

"Until the cities are laid waste and without inhabitant,

The houses are without a man,

The land is utterly desolate,

[12] *The Lord has removed men far away,*

And the forsaken places are many in the midst of the land.

[13] *But yet a tenth will be in it,*

And will return and be for consuming,

As a terebinth tree or as an oak,

Whose stump remains when it is cut down.

So the holy seed shall be its stump."

In willing obedience, Isaiah responds to God's call for a messenger. "Here am I! Send me." God gives him the message. Then Isaiah asks, "How long?" God answers that he will have to preach until the people are all gone and the nation is desolate with only a stump left. Isaiah becomes a wonderful prophet through whom the great Messianic prophecies are revealed. Throughout the book he wrote, he takes us to the cross of the Messiah in Isaiah 53 and then into the kingdom. The man with a dirty mouth was used by God to preach the riches of the Messianic triumph, once the Lord dealt with his sin.

Discussion Questions:

1. What did the death of King Uzziah have to do with the timing of the vision?

2. Should worship of God cause us to evaluate ourselves?

3. What is the connection between counseling and worship?

4. Is there any music in Isaiah 6? What is the significance of it not being mentioned?

5. How can we understand the culture in which we live?

6. How should Christian speech be different from the general culture?

7. Did God tell Isaiah that he wasn't really guilty? Why not?

8. Why is our speech a good indication of our heart?

9. Is numerical and financial success the expected outcome of our Christian service?

10. Why is Isaiah 6:9-10 one of the most quoted passages in the New Testament?

11. What have you learned from this study about God?

12. What have you learned in this study about counseling?

13. What have you learned in this study about yourself?

Chapter Ten:

DANIEL–SHAME

J oe is a patriot. He loves his country. He is constantly upset as he listens to conservative talk radio and Fox News. He is angry with the government for taking the Bible, prayer and morality out of public schools. He believes that there is a conspiracy to compromise the churches also. He comes to you and wants to discuss what is going on in our country. He is ashamed of how many so-called Christians act. What kind of counsel would you give this dear troubled man?

The Problem:

Daniel was a true Israeli patriot. He saw his nation destroyed and knew it was an act of God's judgment. He prayed and God answered him.

What wisdom can we gain from the counsel of the Wonderful Counselor to Daniel?

Daniel 9:1–19 "In the first year of Darius the son of Ahasuerus, of the lineage of the Medes, who was made king over the realm of the Chaldeans — ² in the first year of his reign I, Daniel, understood by the books the number of the years specified by the word of the Lord through Jeremiah the prophet, that He would accomplish seventy years in the desolations of Jerusalem.

³ Then I set my face toward the Lord God to make request by prayer and supplications, with fasting, sackcloth, and ashes. ⁴ And I prayed to the Lord my God, and made confession, and said, "O Lord, great and awesome God, who keeps His covenant and mercy with those who love Him, and with those who keep His commandments, ⁵ we have sinned and committed iniquity, we have done wickedly and rebelled, even by departing from Your precepts and Your judgments. ⁶ Neither have *we heeded Your servants the prophets, who spoke in Your name to our kings and our princes, to our fathers and all the people of the land. ⁷ O Lord, righteousness belongs to You, but to us <u>shame</u> of face, as it is this day—to the men of Judah, to the inhabitants of Jerusalem and all Israel, those near and those far off in all the countries to which You have driven them, because of the unfaithfulness which they have committed against You.*

⁸ "O Lord, to us belongs <u>shame</u> of face, to our kings, our princes, and our fathers, because we have sinned against You. ⁹ To the Lord our God belong mercy and forgiveness, though we have rebelled against Him. ¹⁰ We have not obeyed the voice of the Lord our God, to walk in His laws, which He set before us by His servants the prophets. ¹¹ Yes, all Israel has transgressed Your law, and has departed so as not to obey Your voice; therefore the curse and the oath written in the Law of Moses the servant of God have been poured out on us, because we have sinned against

Him. [12] And He has confirmed His words, which He spoke against us and against our judges who judged us, by bringing upon us a great disaster; for under the whole heaven such has never been done as what has been done to Jerusalem.

[13] "As it is written in the Law of Moses, all this disaster has come upon us; yet we have not made our prayer before the Lord our God, that we might turn from our iniquities and understand Your truth. [14] Therefore the Lord has kept the disaster in mind, and brought it upon us; for the Lord our God is righteous in all the works which He does, though we have not obeyed His voice. [15] And now, O Lord our God, who brought Your people out of the land of Egypt with a mighty hand, and made Yourself a name, as it is this day—we have sinned, we have done wickedly!

[16] "O Lord, according to all Your righteousness, I pray, let Your anger and Your fury be turned away from Your city Jerusalem, Your holy mountain;

because for our sins, and for the iniquities of our fathers, Jerusalem and Your people are a reproach to all those around us. ¹⁷ Now therefore, our God, hear the prayer of Your servant, and his supplications, and for the Lord's sake cause Your face to shine on Your sanctuary, which is desolate. ¹⁸ O my God, incline Your ear and hear; open Your eyes and see our desolations, and the city which is called by Your name; for we do not present our supplications before You because of our righteous deeds, but because of Your great mercies. ¹⁹ O Lord, hear! O Lord, forgive! O Lord, listen and act! Do not delay for Your own sake, my God, for Your city and Your people are called by Your name."

Daniel was ashamed of his nation. In Daniel 9:7-8 we read: "O Lord, righteousness belongs to you, … but to us shame of face, to our kings, our princes and our fathers, because we have sinned against You." Daniel's prayer of identification with his people and the shame they felt was an expression of humility and concern for Israel's future. Much like our Lord's model prayer in which he taught his disciples to pray, "forgive us our trespasses", Daniel identified with the shame of his people. But he also was genuinely ashamed of the sins and failures of his nation. Shame is a good thing for a counselee to feel if their consciences have been biblically trained and the Holy Spirit is convicting them.

The Counsel:

Daniel 10:10–19 "Suddenly, a hand touched me, which made me tremble on my knees and on the palms of my hands. [11] And he said to me, <u>"O Daniel, man greatly beloved, understand the words that I speak to you, and stand upright, for I have now been sent to you."</u> While he was speaking this word to me, I stood trembling.

[12] Then he said to me, <u>"Do not fear, Daniel, for from the first day that you set your heart to understand, and to humble yourself before your God,</u>

your words were heard; and I have come because of your words. ¹³ But the prince of the kingdom of Persia withstood me twenty-one days; and behold, Michael, one of the chief princes, came to help me, for I had been left alone there with the kings of Persia. ¹⁴ Now I have come to make you understand what will happen to your people in the latter days, for the vision refers to many days yet to come."

¹⁵ When he had spoken such words to me, I turned my face toward the ground and became speechless. ¹⁶ And suddenly, one having the likeness of the sons of men touched my lips; then I opened my mouth and spoke, saying to him who stood before me, "My lord, because of the vision my sorrows have overwhelmed me, and I have retained no strength. ¹⁷ For how can this servant of my lord talk with you, my lord? As for me, no strength remains in me now, nor is any breath left in me."

¹⁸ Then again, the one having the likeness of a man touched me and strengthened me. ¹⁹ <u>And he said, "O man greatly beloved, fear not! Peace be to you; be strong, yes, be strong!"</u>

So when he spoke to me I was strengthened, and said, "Let my lord speak, for you have strengthened me."

God sent an angel to give Daniel skill in understanding (Daniel 9:22). God revealed His plan for Israel and then after Daniel prayed again, God sent an angel again to encourage him. The angel told Daniel that he was greatly loved and that he should not fear (10:11-12). Then the angel again revealed details of God's prophetic plan for Israel.

The Outcome:

Daniel was strengthened (10:18-19). Daniel learned to understand what is in the Scripture of Truth (10:21). He is told to go his way until the end;

for he will rest, and will arise to his inheritance at the end of days (12:13).

Discussion Questions:

1. How did Daniel find out that the Babylonian Captivity of Israel would only last 70 years?

2. Did Daniel include himself when he confessed the sins of his nation? Why?

3. Did Daniel conclude that his nation deserved the desolations of captivity? Why?

4. How can we counsel our people when they become angry about what is happening to our country?

5. How important is Bible Prophecy in understanding what is going on in the world today?

6. What benefits did Daniel receive personally from the counsel God gave him?

7. What have you learned from this study about God?

8. What have you learned from this study about counseling?

9. What have you learned from this study about yourself?

Chapter Eleven:

THE WOMAN AT THE WELL – EMPTINESS

P atsy was living with a new guy. He had a lot of baggage, but so did she. Five marriages had started well and ended badly. She liked men and they liked her, but none of them could meet her inner longing for love, joy and peace. In fact, she had given up on ever having her empty heart filled with love.

When Jesus had sent the disciples into that Samaritan town to find some lunch, He sat down by the well outside of town. A woman came to draw water. The encounter that ensued reveals the skills of the Wonderful Counselor.

John 4:1–34 Therefore, when the Lord knew that the Pharisees had heard that Jesus made and baptized more disciples than John [2] (though Jesus Himself did not baptize, but His disciples), [3] He left Judea and departed again to Galilee. [4] But He needed to go through Samaria.

[5] So He came to a city of Samaria which is called Sychar, near the plot of ground that Jacob gave to his son Joseph. [6] Now Jacob's well was there. Jesus therefore, being wearied from His journey, sat thus by the well. It was about the sixth hour.

[7] A woman of Samaria came to draw water. <u>Jesus said to her, "Give Me a drink."</u> [8] For His disciples had gone away into the city to buy food.

[9] Then the woman of Samaria said to Him, "How is it that You, being a Jew, ask a drink from me, a Samaritan woman?" For Jews have no dealings with Samaritans.

[10] <u>Jesus answered and said to her, "If you knew the gift of God, and who it is who says to you,</u>

'Give Me a drink,' you would have asked Him, and He would have given you living water."

¹¹ The woman said to Him, "Sir, You have nothing to draw with, and the well is deep. Where then do You get that living water? ¹² Are You greater than our father Jacob, who gave us the well, and drank from it himself, as well as his sons and his livestock?"

¹³ Jesus answered and said to her, "Whoever drinks of this water will thirst again, ¹⁴ but whoever drinks of the water that I shall give him will never thirst. But the water that I shall give him will become in him a fountain of water springing up into everlasting life."

¹⁵ The woman said to Him, "Sir, give me this water, that I may not thirst, nor come here to draw."

¹⁶ Jesus said to her, "Go, call your husband, and come here."

¹⁷ *The woman answered and said, "I have no husband."*

Jesus said to her, "You have well said, 'I have no husband,' ¹⁸ for you have had five husbands, and the one whom you now have is not your husband; in that you spoke truly."

¹⁹ *The woman said to Him, "Sir, I perceive that You are a prophet. ²⁰ Our fathers worshiped on this mountain, and you Jews say that in Jerusalem is the place where one ought to worship."*

²¹ *Jesus said to her, "Woman, believe Me, the hour is coming when you will neither on this mountain, nor in Jerusalem, worship the Father. ²² You worship what you do not know; we know what we worship, for salvation is of the Jews. ²³ But the hour is coming, and now is, when the true worshipers will worship the Father in spirit and truth; for the Father is seeking such to worship*

Him. <u>24 God is Spirit, and those who worship Him</u> <u>*must worship in spirit and truth.*"</u>

25 The woman said to Him, "I know that Messiah is coming" (who is called Christ). "When He comes, He will tell us all things."

<u>*26 Jesus said to her, "I who speak to you am He."*</u>

27 And at this point His disciples came, and they marveled that He talked with a woman; yet no one said, "What do You seek?" or, "Why are You talking with her?"

28 The woman then left her waterpot, went her way into the city, and said to the men, 29 "Come, see a Man who told me all things that I ever did. Could this be the Christ?" 30 Then they went out of the city and came to Him.

31 In the meantime His disciples urged Him, saying, "Rabbi, eat."

<u>³² But He said to them, "I have food to eat of which you do not know."</u>

³³ Therefore the disciples said to one another, "Has anyone brought Him anything to eat?"

<u>³⁴ Jesus said to them, "My food is to do the will of Him who sent Me, and to finish His work.</u>

<u>The Problem:</u>

This lady had had five husbands and the man she was currently living with was not her husband. She came alone to the well. She was well educated and opinionated. She was a member of a despised group of people. Her real need was a spiritual thirst that she had tried to satisfy with human relationships.

Many are looking for love, peace and joy in human relationships today only to find that everyone else is looking for the same thing and not finding it.

The Counsel:

Jesus broke down the cultural and religious barriers by asking her to give him a drink of water. When she asked Him how He, as a Jewish man, could ask her, a Samaritan woman, for a drink of water, she began realizing that she was not dealing with an ordinary Jew. Jesus probed right to her deepest spiritual need. "If you knew the gift of God, and who it is who says to you, "Give me a drink," you would have asked Him, and He would have given you living water". Later Jesus went on to say, "the water that I will give him will become a fountain of living water springing up into everlasting life."

Jesus knew her life situation and told her that He knew she had had five husbands and that the one she had now was not her husband. Jesus had incredible insight into her life. We, too, can have wisdom from God when we counsel. James 1:5 "If any of you lacks wisdom, let him ask of God, who gives to all liberally and without reproach, and it will be given to him." John 14:12–14 *"Most assuredly, I say to you, he who believes in Me, the works that I do he will do also; and greater works than these he will do, because I go to My Father. ¹³ And whatever you ask in My name, that I will do, that the Father may be glorified in the Son. ¹⁴ If you ask anything in My name, I will do it."* The Wonderful Counselor will give you amazing insights into people's problems if you ask Him in faith (James 1:5-8). Jesus is our example because He laid aside the independent use of his attributes as God while ministering on earth. (Philippians 2:7). We can do what He did in our counseling because we have the Word of God and the Spirit of God. The Spirit of God uses the Word of God to enable us to be competent to counsel one another (Romans 15:14 and Colossians 3:16).

The Outcome:

When Jesus told the woman at the well that He was the promised Messiah (John 4:26), she left her waterpot and went into her city. She told the men, "Come, see a man who told me all things that I ever did. Could this be the Christ?" The town men came out with her to meet Jesus. His insight into her need and past convinced her to believe in Jesus.

God can give you, as a Christian counselor, insight into people's needs that goes way beyond psychological analysis. And Jesus felt the deep satisfaction that comes to the Christian counselor when a person comes to know Christ. "My food is to do the will of Him who sent me and to finish His work" (John 4:34). Jesus shows us that the satisfaction of the deepest longings of the human heart is not for marriage or food and drink, but for the love, joy and peace that comes from fellowship with God through His Son, Jesus Christ.

Discussion Questions:

1. Why did Jesus need to go through Samaria? Is there some geographical area near you that people generally avoid?

2. Why did Jesus ask the woman for a drink instead of offering to draw water for her?

3. Why did Jesus talk about living water? Why doesn't Jesus ever present the gospel in the same way?

4. Why did Jesus tell the woman to go and call her husband to come there?

5. How did Jesus answer her question about where to worship? How would you answer someone who asked you where they should go to church?

6. What was more satisfying to Jesus than eating?

7. What did the disciples learn from this event?

8. What counsel would you gain from this event that would help you counsel a person with an eating disorder?

9. What have you learned from this study about God?

10. What have you learned from this study about counseling?

11. What have you learned from this study about yourself?

Chapter Twelve:

THE RICH YOUNG RULER– MATERIALISM

J oseph is a fine young man. He wants to join your church and since you are on the membership committee, he asks you a question, "What must I do to be a member of your church?" How will you answer him? How did Jesus answer the rich young ruler who came to him?

Matthew 19:16–26 (Mark 10:17–27;
Luke 18:18–27)

¹⁶ Now behold, one came and said to Him, "Good Teacher, what good thing shall I do that I may have eternal life?"

<u>¹⁷ So He said to him, "Why do you call Me good? No one is good but One, that is, God. But if you want to enter into life, keep the commandments."</u>

<u>¹⁸ He said to Him, "Which ones?"</u>

<u>Jesus said, "'You shall not murder,' 'You shall not commit adultery,' 'You shall not steal,' 'You shall not bear false witness,' ¹⁹ 'Honor your father and your mother,' and, 'You shall love your neighbor as yourself.'"</u>

²⁰ The young man said to Him, "All these things I have kept from my youth. What do I still lack?"

<u>²¹ Jesus said to him, "If you want to be perfect, go, sell what you have and give to the poor, and you will have treasure in heaven; and come, follow Me."</u>

²² But when the young man heard that saying, he went away sorrowful, for he had great possessions.

²³ Then Jesus said to His disciples, "Assuredly, I say to you that it is hard for a rich man to enter the kingdom of heaven. ²⁴ And again I say to you, it is easier for a camel to go through the eye of a needle than for a rich man to enter the kingdom of God."

²⁵ When His disciples heard it, they were greatly astonished, saying, "Who then can be saved?"

²⁶ But Jesus looked at them and said to them, "With men this is impossible, but with God all things are possible."

The Problem:

This young man had a question: "Good Teacher, what good thing shall I do that I may have eternal life?" Apparently he believed that he could enter Heaven by good works and morality. He appeared to be a very self-confident person. His question then was, "What do I lack?" He couldn't think of anything that he had left undone. When confronted with six of the Ten Commandments that related to his fellow man, the young man replied, "All these things I have kept from my youth." He didn't think he had any problem at all. He thought other people had problems because they were not as good as he was. These are the most difficult people to counsel because they think the other people in their lives need help, but they do not. What would Jesus do? What approach would He take? What would you do?

The Counsel:

Jesus pointed this young man to God, not man, as the measure of what is "good". In verse 17 we read, *"So He said to him, "Why do you call Me good? No one is good but One, that is, God."*

Then Jesus pointed him to the law of God contained in the Ten Commandments: *"But if you want to enter into life, keep the commandments."*

18 He said to Him, "Which ones?"

Jesus said, "'You shall not murder,' 'You shall not commit adultery,' 'You shall not steal,' 'You shall not bear false witness,' [19] 'Honor your father and your mother,' and, 'You shall love your neighbor as yourself.'"

The young man responded to the six commands relating to his fellow man by saying, "All these things I have kept from my youth. What do I still lack?"

It didn't appear that Jesus was getting anywhere with this young man. The final counsel pointed out this young man's sin: covetousness – the tenth commandment: In verse 21 Jesus said to him, ***"If you want to be perfect, go, sell what you have and give to the poor, and you will have treasure in heaven; and come, follow Me."***

If a person wanted to be good enough to go to Heaven by good works, how good would that person need to be? Jesus said they would have to be perfect. He said the same thing in Matthew 5:48, ***"Therefore you shall be perfect, just as your***

Father in heaven is perfect." Theoretically, a person could get to Heaven by being good, but they would have to be as good as God. So, practically, that is not the way to obtain eternal life.

The Response:

The Scripture says in verse 22 that he went away sorrowful, because he had great possessions. Though counseled by Jesus Himself, this young man was not ready to realize that he could not fulfill the law himself. Jesus was not attempting to get this man saved yet. Jesus was first seeking to get this man lost. Before anyone can be saved, they must know that they are lost. For that reason Jesus spent so much time in His ministry showing the heart of the Law, as he did in Matthew 5-7. Jesus was showing people what the law could not do, because of the moral weakness of fallen flesh. Jesus met a lot of people whom He did not help. It was not due to some flaw in the Wonderful Counselor. The problem was with the counselee. In Matthew

9:12-13 we read, *"When Jesus heard that, He said to them, "Those who are well have no need of a physician, but those who are sick. ¹³ But go and learn what this means: 'I desire mercy and not sacrifice.' For I did not come to call the righteous, but sinners, to repentance."*

Jesus then used this encounter to teach his disciples: In verse 23 we read, *"Then Jesus said to His disciples, "Assuredly, I say to you that it is hard for a rich man to enter the kingdom of heaven. ²⁴ And again I say to you, it is easier for a camel to go through the eye of a needle than for a rich man to enter the kingdom of God."*

²⁵ When His disciples heard it, they were greatly astonished, saying, "Who then can be saved?"

²⁶ But Jesus looked at them and said to them, "With men this is impossible, but with God all things are possible."

Jesus pointed out to them that rich men can only enter Heaven "with God". Without God they cannot be saved.

The Consequences:

This rich young ruler went away sorrowful. He was rich in this world's goods but without eternal life. How sad! In our counseling, we must realize that some counselees could not have been helped even by the Lord Himself. The problem is that they do not think they have a problem. We can pray for them and be patient with them. Perhaps the Lord will bring circumstances into their lives that will humble them: *2 Timothy 2:24–26 "And a servant of the Lord must not quarrel but be gentle to all, able to teach, patient, ²⁵ in humility correcting those who are in opposition, if God perhaps will grant them repentance, so that they may know the truth, ²⁶ and that they may come to their senses and escape the snare of the devil, having been taken captive by him to do his will."*

Discussion Questions:

1. How did Jesus define the word, "good"?

2. Why did Jesus bring the Mosaic law into the discussion?

3. How can you use the Ten Commandments in your counseling?

4. What was the root problem of this young man?

5. How would you describe the counseling techniques Jesus used with this young man?

6. How did God show you that your good works did not entitle you to eternal life?

7. What have you learned about God from this study?

8. What have you learned about counseling from this study?

9. What have you learned about yourself from this study?

Chapter Thirteen:

THE WOMAN CAUGHT IN ADULTERY

The Facebook account and the emails he discovered made it clear to Harry that his wife Clara was in an adulterous affair with his best friend, Tom. He angrily confronted her with the evidence. She was really sorry, but Harry couldn't forgive her. He had never committed adultery. How could she do such a thing? He would never forgive her! Divorce was the only option. Because they were Christians, they came to you for counsel. How would you start?

Jesus was confronted by Scribes and Pharisees with a woman who had been caught in the very act of adultery. How did he counsel them and her?

John 8:2–11 "Now early in the morning He came again into the temple, and all the people came to Him; and He sat down and taught them. ³ Then the scribes and Pharisees brought to Him a woman caught in adultery. And when they had set her in the midst, ⁴ they said to Him, "Teacher, this woman was caught in adultery, in the very act. ⁵ Now Moses, in the law, commanded us that such should be stoned. But what do You say?" ⁶ This they said, testing Him, that they might have something of which to accuse Him. But Jesus stooped down and wrote on the ground with His finger, as though He did not hear.

⁷ So when they continued asking Him, He raised Himself up and said to them, "He who is without sin among you, let him throw a stone at her first." ⁸ And again He stooped down and wrote on the ground. ⁹ Then those who heard it, being convicted by their conscience, went out one by one, beginning with the oldest even to the last. And Jesus was left alone, and the woman standing in

139

*the midst. <u>**¹⁰ When Jesus had raised Himself up and saw no one but the woman, He said to her, "Woman, where are those accusers of yours? Has no one condemned you?"**</u>*

¹¹ She said, "No one, Lord."

<u>*And Jesus said to her, "Neither do I condemn you; go and sin no more."*</u>

<u>The Problem:</u>

Early in the morning, in the Temple, the Scribes and Pharisees brought to Jesus a woman who had been caught in the act of adultery. They cited the law of Moses which called for stoning in such a case. They then asked what He would say.

Sometimes both an accuser and the accused will come to you for counsel. How will you handle it?

The Counsel:

Jesus dealt with the accusers by writing on the ground with His finger as though He did not hear. He waited until they continued to ask Him the question, then He stood up and said, "He who is without sin among you, let him throw a stone at her first." He stooped down and wrote on the ground again. The accusers left one at a time, oldest to youngest. Jesus rose up and asked the woman, "Where are those accusers of yours? Has no one condemned you? She answered, "No one, Lord." Jesus then said to her, "Neither do I condemn you; go and sin no more."

Paul expands on this idea in ***Titus 2:11–14 and 3:9 For the grace of God that brings salvation has appeared to all men, *** [12] ***teaching us that, denying ungodliness and worldly lusts, we should live soberly, righteously, and godly in the present age,*** [13] ***looking for the blessed hope and glorious appearing of our great God and Savior Jesus Christ,*** [14] ***who gave Himself for us, that He might redeem us from*** *every lawless deed and purify for Himself His own special people, zealous for good works.*

⁹ But avoid foolish disputes, genealogies, contentions, and strivings about the law; for they are unprofitable and useless.

Jesus demonstrated what Paul taught. Grace teaches us to live holy lives. Grace also teaches us to not be judgmental of others.

The Outcome:

We have no record of this woman's response, but the consequence is that she was not stoned to death and her accusers were denied their desire to humiliate Jesus with this case.

Discussion Questions:

1. Why was this woman brought to Jesus?

2. What do you think Jesus wrote on the ground?

3. Why did Jesus get rid of this lady's accusers?

4. How would you deal with a person who comes to you to accuse another person?

5. Why do you think the oldest ones left first?

6. How should we counsel adulterers and adulteresses?

7. What do you think Jesus meant when he said: "Neither do I condemn you"?

8. What do you see behind Jesus counsel to "Go and sin no more."

9. What have you learned about God from this study?

10. What have you learned about counseling from this study?

11. What have you learned about yourself from this study?

Chapter Fourteen:

THOMAS–SKEPTICISM

I was asked to visit Charles in the hospital. He was dying of leukemia. He had studied comparative religions in college and had come to the conclusion that religion was good because it made people act morally, but he saw no more truth in Christianity than in any other religion. He told me, "I would like to believe in God. I would like to believe in heaven. But I don't." Rather than arguing with Charles, I proposed an experiment. "Read the Gospel of John, one chapter a day. Before reading, pray a prayer like this, 'God, if you are there, please reveal Yourself to me as I read.'" He agreed to do it. I came back into the room a week later and I could see the joy on his face. He said, "I believe!" I had not argued with him. But the self-authenticating Word of God in the Gospel of John had been used by God to do what it had been written to do. *John 20:31 but these are written that you may believe that Jesus is the Christ, the Son of God, and that believing you may have life in His name.*

John 20:24–31 "Now Thomas, called the Twin, one of the twelve, was not with them when Jesus came. ²⁵ The other disciples therefore said to him, "We have seen the Lord." So he said to them, "Unless I see in His hands the print of the nails, and put my finger into the print of the nails, and put my hand into His side, I will not believe." ²⁶ And after eight days His disciples were again inside, and Thomas with them. Jesus came, the doors being shut, and stood in the midst, and said, "Peace to you!" ²⁷ Then He said to Thomas, "Reach your finger here, and look at My hands; and reach your hand here, and put it into My side. Do not be unbelieving, but believing." ²⁸ And Thomas answered and said to Him, "My Lord and my God!" ²⁹ Jesus said to him, "Thomas, because you have seen Me, you have believed. Blessed are those who have not seen and yet have believed." ³⁰ And truly Jesus did many other signs in the presence of His disciples, which are not written in this book; ³¹ but these are written that you may believe that Jesus is the Christ, the Son of God, and that believing you may have life in His name.

The Problem:

Thomas missed assembling with his fellow believers. We read in Hebrews 10:23–25 *"Let us hold fast the confession of our hope without wavering, for He who promised is faithful. ²⁴ And let us consider one another in order to stir up love and good works, ²⁵ not forsaking the assembling of ourselves together, as is the manner of some, but exhorting one another, and so much the more as you see the Day approaching."*

Thomas required evidence for faith. He was unwilling to believe just because others told him that Jesus was risen.

The Counsel:

Jesus willingly supplied Thomas with the evidence that he requested. John 20:27: *"Then He said to Thomas, "Reach your finger here, and look at My hands; and reach your hand here, and put it into My side. Do not be unbelieving, but believing."*

Then Jesus blessed those who have not seen and yet have believed: *"Jesus said to him, "Thomas, because you have seen Me, you have believed. Blessed are those who have not seen and yet have believed."*

The Apostle John then summed up the reason for writing his book, the Gospel of John, by saying that he recorded the signs Jesus performed so that the readers would believe in Him.

So we see two factors that will help a person maintain faith in the midst of a skeptical world: Christian fellowship and the study of God's Word, the Bible. Faith comes by hearing and hearing by the Word of God (Romans 10:17).

1 Peter 1:6–9 "In this you greatly rejoice, though now for a little while, if need be, you have been grieved by various trials, ⁷ that the genuineness of your faith, being much more precious than gold that perishes, though it is tested by fire, may be found to praise, honor, and glory at the revelation of Jesus Christ, ⁸ whom having not seen you love. Though now you do not see Him, yet believing, you rejoice with joy inexpressible and full of glory, ⁹ receiving the end of your faith—the salvation of your souls."

Faith that has been tested is healthy and mature. Without faith we cannot please God (Hebrews 11:6). Faith is necessary for salvation according to Acts 16:30-31: *"And he brought them out and said, "Sirs, what must I do to be saved?" ³¹ So they said, "Believe on the Lord Jesus Christ, and you will be saved, you and your household."*

Faith is an honest response to the evidence. The evidence for the truthfulness of Christianity is in the documents that have been handed down to us from the eyewitnesses of the actual events. Faith is not a "leap in the dark". It is the conclusion of a heart and mind that is willing to submit to God. Submission is a work that only God can do in us.

The Outcome:

Thomas overcame his initial skepticism and not only believed, but he worshipped: *John 20:28: "And Thomas answered and said to Him, "My Lord and my God!"* Here we see that true faith results in worship.

Discussion Questions:

1. Why do you think Thomas failed to meet with the disciples the previous Sunday night?

2. Why do some people seem to lose their faith?

3. Is there a link between moral failure and skepticism?

4. Have you ever had doubts about the truthfulness of Christianity? How did you resolve them?

5. What evidence for Christian faith is most convincing to you?

6. How are faith and worship related in your experience?

7. Does daily Bible reading help to strengthen your faith?

8. What have you learned from this study about God?

9. What have you learned from this study about counseling?

10. What have you learned from this study about yourself?

Chapter Fifteen:

PETER–DEPRESSION

P ete had been a pastor, but now he just felt like a failure. He had done so well, but when arrested and interrogated, he folded. He signed the statement that repudiated his Christian faith and now his captors had published it in all the newspapers. How could he face his fellow pastors? How could he face his congregation? He had not lost his faith in the Lord, but he had lost faith in himself. He wanted to crawl into a hole and die. He had given up on life. Maybe he could just go back to his old job and forget the whole thing. What was he to do?

John 21:15-19 "When they had finished breakfast, Jesus said to Simon Peter, "Simon, son of John, do you love me more than these?" He said to him, "Yes, Lord; you know that I love you." He said to him, "Feed my lambs." ¹⁶ He said to him a second time, "Simon, son of John, do you love me?" He said to him, "Yes, Lord; you know that I love you." He said to him, "Tend my sheep." ¹⁷ He said to him the third time, "Simon, son of John, do you love me?" Peter was grieved because he said to him the third time, "Do you love me?" and he said to him, "Lord, you know everything; you know that I love you." Jesus said to him, "Feed my sheep. ¹⁸ Truly, truly, I say to you, when you were young, you used to dress yourself and walk wherever you wanted, but when you are old, you will stretch out your hands, and another will dress you and carry you where you do not want to go." ¹⁹ (This he said to show by what kind of death he was to glorify God.) And after saying this he said to him, "Follow me."

The Problem:

Peter had boasted that he would never deny the Lord. He would die first, he said. He attacked

153

the High Priest's servant and cut off his ear. But from that point on, things went downhill fast. He fled with the others when Jesus allowed Himself to be arrested. Then he denied Jesus three times before the rooster crowed just as Jesus had said he would. Now Jesus is risen. Peter took five other disciples back to fishing. But after a long night of not catching any fish, they saw Jesus on the shore. When he told them to fish on the other side of the boat they caught lots of fish. Peter jumped in the water and when the boat and disciples arrived, they all ate the breakfast Jesus had cooked for them. After breakfast Jesus wanted to talk to Peter. What would he say? Would he tell Peter that he is now disqualified? Would he rebuke him?

The Counsel:

Jesus asked him a question three times in different ways "Simon, son of Jonah, Do you love me more than these?" "Simon, son of Jonah, do you love me?"

Jesus gave him an assignment three times in different ways: "Feed my lambs". "Tend my sheep." "Feed my sheep."

After telling him that he would live long enough to require assistance with walking and dressing himself, Jesus gave Peter a command: "Follow Me". Our love for Christ is the greatest motivation we could ever have for serving Him.

The Outcome:

On the Day of Pentecost, Peter preached to the multitudes of people that Jesus was the Son of God and that He had risen from the dead. Three thousand Jews from all over the world got saved. Peter knew that Jesus had forgiven and restored him. The Holy Spirit could have chosen one of the disciples who had a "squeaky clean" record, but Peter was chosen to preach that day. God chooses the foolish things of this world to confound the wise: *1 Corinthians 1:25–31 Because the foolishness of God is wiser than men, and the weakness of God is stronger than men.* [26] *For you see your calling, brethren, that not many wise according to the flesh, not many mighty, not many noble, are called.* [27] *But God has chosen the foolish things of the world to put to shame the wise, and God has chosen the weak things of the world to put to shame the things which are mighty;* [28] *and the base things of the world and the things which are despised God has chosen, and the things which are not, to bring to nothing the things that are,* [29] *that no flesh should glory in His presence.* [30] *But of Him you are in Christ Jesus, who became for us wisdom from God—and righteousness and sanctification and redemption—* [31] *that, as it is written, "He who glories, let him glory in the Lord."*

Discussion Questions:

1. Why did Jesus wait until after breakfast to talk with Peter?

2. Why did Jesus use his old name: Simon?

3. Why did Jesus remind Peter that he was Jonah's son?

4. Why did Jesus ask Peter if he loved Jesus?

5. Why did Jesus ask the same basic question three times?

6. What is the significance of Jesus' use of the words "lambs" and "sheep"?

7. What have you learned about God from this study?

8. What have you learned about counseling from this study?

9. What have you learned about yourself from this study?

Chapter Sixteen:

PAUL – AFFLICTION

S teve was so frustrated! He had been to every doctor he could think of and they all told him the same thing. There was nothing more they could do. How could he live like this? He prayed that God would deliver him three times. But nothing changed. It seemed like God was not listening.

2 Corinthians 12:7–10 "And lest I should be exalted above measure by the abundance of the revelations, a thorn in the flesh was given to me, a messenger of Satan to buffet me, lest I be exalted above measure. ⁸ *Concerning this thing I pleaded with the Lord three times that it might depart from me.* ⁹ <u>*And He said to me, "My grace is sufficient for you, for My strength is made perfect in weakness."*</u> *Therefore most gladly I will rather boast in my infirmities, that the power of Christ may rest upon me. ¹⁰ Therefore I take pleasure in infirmities, in reproaches, in needs, in persecutions, in distresses, for Christ's sake. For when I am weak, then I am strong."*

The Problem:

Paul had a humbling thorn in the flesh. It was delivered by Satan and it pounded him. He prayed three times for God to take it away. God didn't remove Paul's thorn. In the days of sailing ships, the bottom of the boat had to be filled with heavy items in order for the sails to move the ship forward properly. The Wonderful Counselor wanted Paul to have some "ballast" in the ship of his life to counter the powerful uplift of Paul's journey to the third Heaven. His thorn was designed to hold him down.

When we have wonderful answers to prayer or are greatly used by God, we often need some heavy problems to keep our feet on the ground lest we be lifted up in pride and fall into the condemnation of the Devil (1 Timothy 3:6). God gives us as much victory as He can trust us with since He is our Father and we are His children through faith in Jesus Christ.

The Counsel:

The Lord chose not to remove the thorn, but rather to give Paul grace sufficient to bear it. In fact he would be strengthened in his weakness by the sufficient grace that God would give him. God knows what we need. Our lives are designed by God to be a testimony to His greatness, not ours.

The Response:

Paul understood. He boasted in his infirmities so the power of Christ would rest on him. He took pleasure in infirmities, reproaches, in needs, persecutions and distresses (2 Corinthians 12:10). He learned that he was spiritually strongest when he was otherwise weak. Paul did not delight in the pain itself, but in the power that God gave him in the midst of pain and weakness. The progress of the gospel was the excitement of Paul's life. He saw his problems as "pulpits" for the gospel. He saw his interruptions as opportunities to witness.

The Outcome:

Paul, even with his thorn, continued to serve Christ. He finished well: *2 Timothy 4:6–8, "For I am already being poured out as a drink offering, and the time of my departure is at hand. ⁷ I have fought the good fight, I have finished the race, I have kept the faith. ⁸ Finally, there is laid up for me the crown of righteousness, which the Lord, the righteous Judge, will give to me on that Day, and not to me only but also to all who have loved His appearing."*

He eventually lost his thorn when he was executed and went to Heaven. We do not always have our prayers for healing answered in this life. But we can trust God to do what is best when we ask Him.

Discussion Questions:

1. What do you think Paul's thorn was?

2. How does Satan buffet Christians today?

3. How should you pray about your thorns?

4. How would you counsel someone who thought he was oppressed by demons?

5. How is God's grace sufficient for your thorns?

6. What infirmities has God used in your life?

7. How determined are you to finish well?

8. What have you learned about God from this study?

9. What have you learned about counseling from this study?

10. What have you learned about yourself from this study?

LEADERS' GUIDE

Always begin with prayer. Read the verses or have them read them silently. Summarize the meaning of the passage. Then ask the discussion questions. Wait for group members to respond. After they have shared their ideas, share these answers and your own observations. After answering the discussion questions, review the memory verse for that lesson. Ask your students to work on memorizing the verses. Review verses at the beginning of the next class. End the session with prayer for grace to put these ideas into action in your own lives and ministries.

Chapter One: Cain
Discussion Questions:

1. Why did God respect Abel's offering but not Cain's?

Abel's offering was the firstborn and fat of the flock and involved a blood sacrifice. He offered it in faith according to Hebrews 11:4.

Cain's offering was the fruit of the ground and did not involve blood or faith.

2. How do you think Cain's face looked when his countenance fell while he was very angry?

Have students try to demonstrate by making angry looking faces. Vote on who makes the most convincing angry face.

3. Is there a link between anger and depression?

Anger that is not dealt with properly can build into depression over time. Anger is often a secondary emotion covering a more vulnerable first emotion. Cain had his feelings hurt by not being

accepted and being jealous of his brother's acceptance. He then converted all this "raw" emotion to
anger. God shows Cain how to reverse this down-
ward spiral into sin.

4. Is there a link between depression and violence?

Depression can lead to violence if a person
blames someone for their problems. Anger becomes
bitterness and bitterness can erupt in violence.

5. Why do you think God asked Cain so many questions?

God wanted Cain to think about himself and
his anger.

6. Why did God give Cain two options? Why not just tell him what to do?

God respects the authority He has given us to
make decisions and to live with the consequences.

7. What insight did the Lord share with Cain? How would you use this phrase in counseling someone?

The Lord shared the insight that sin desired to have him but that he should rule over it. We could show a counselee that his or her sin desires to rule their life but that God wants them to rule over sin and be victorious over it. They have a choice. 1 Corinthians 10:13 assures believers that we do not have to sin.

8. What do you think Cain said to Abel before he killed him?

Probably, "I hate you". He who hates is brother is a murderer (1 John 3:15).

9. How might this story have turned out differently?

Let students give possible outcomes if Cain had repented of his sinful anger and reconciled with his brother, Abel.

10. What good did God's counseling do for Cain?

Not much, because he didn't listen to it.

11. What did you learn about God from this study?

God is a patient counselor. He respects the authority of people to choose their own way. He continued to help Cain even after he rejected God's counsel.

12. What have you learned about counseling from this study?

Some counselees will not listen, even if they were to have a perfect counselor like the Lord Himself, the Wonderful Counselor. We also learn how rejection leads to anger, which leads to depression and possibly violence. We learn the importance of non-verbal cues (Cain's face fell). We learn the importance of asking good questions that make people think. We see the importance of showing options instead of just telling people what to do. God offered deep insights.

13. What did you learn about yourself from this study?

Share about your struggles with anger, depression or violence.

Memory verse for Chapter One:
Ephesians 4:26-27

BE AWGY AND SIN Not LET NotTHKSUN

Chapter Two: Hagar
Discussion Questions:

1. How would you have counseled Sarai when she seemed to be infertile?

You could discuss various ethical options for infertility treatments. If that has been pursued, you could discuss adoption or helping parents with their children (nephews and nieces, etc.).

2. How would you have conducted marriage counseling with Abram and Sarai in this conflict over Hagar despising Sarai?

It is complicated due to plural marriage and slavery issues. You probably should address headship and submission on the part of Abram and Sarai.

3. Is there ever a time to send an abused wife back to an abusive situation?

If a crime has been committed, the police should be called in and charges filed. Sometimes we have not heard the whole story, only one side. Seek to meet with the alleged abuser and seek God's wisdom to ascertain what and when to seek restoration of the relationship through humility, confession, forgiveness and cooperation. (Ephesians 5:15-33 and 1 Peter 3:1-6 would be good passages to consider with them.) Check with local ordinances as to reporting requirements. Consider legal counsel. Be sure to have insurance coverage for your counseling ministry.

4. Why do you think the Lord asked Hagar where she had come from?

He wanted her to think about the family situation she had left behind and how she had responded to it.

5. Why do you think the Lord asked Hagar where she was going?

He wanted her to consider the consequences of her actions.

6. What did Hagar learn about God?

He sees. He hears. He helps.

7. According to Genesis 21:17, what was Hagar's problem?

Her root problem was fear. How can we help fearful people? 2 Timothy 1:7 tells us that fear does not come from God. The formula for overcoming fear is found in Isaiah 41:10. As our understanding of His love for us increases our abnormal fears decrease (1 John 4:18).

8. How can we help people open their eyes to see God's solutions?

We can teach them to understand their lives in light of the Scriptures.

9. What have you learned about God from this study?

God is the one Who sees, hears and helps us in our troubles, even if we have gotten ourselves into it.

10. What have you learned about counseling from this study?

To ask "thought questions", to give direction to those who are open to it, to give encouragement and hope, and to pray that your counselee will have insight.

11. What have you learned about yourself from this study?

Share about your need for patience with those who are abused. Share fears that have hindered you from submitting to authorities in your life and how you overcame them. Share the joy of restored relationships with authorities in your life.

Memory Verse for Chapter Two: 1 Peter 3:6

Chapter Three: Job
Discussion Questions:

1. Why did God allow Satan to do such terrible things to Job?

To answer Satan's accusation found in Job 1:6-12 and 2:1-7.

To refine Job as gold. (Job 23:10)

2. What are some ways that Satan can attack Christians?

Through losses of wealth, health and family.

3. Are losses always the result of sins in our lives?

No. Jesus made this clear in John 9:1-3.

4. Why did God ask Job so many questions?

He wanted him to think deeply about Who God is and who Job is.

5. Why did God take Job to the "Zoo" and "Planetarium"?

Many verses in Job describe the creation God has made and that He upholds. This discription was designed to show Job that God is so much greater than finite human beings. God speaks very directly in the book of Job about His creation.

6. How can we know what God is doing with people so we don't give wrong counsel like Job's counselors did?

Ask God for wisdom as found in James 1:5.

7. How important is reconciliation in dealing with grief?

Broken relationships complicate grief and can infect the wounds of the soul with bitterness. Helping grieving people to reconcile with God and with loved ones goes a long way toward helping them heal.

8. How can we help people to be reconciled to loved ones and God when they are grieving?

Teach them to speak honestly and lovingly in spite of their grief. Sometimes letters help because the counselee and counselor can discuss the communication before sending it.

9. What have we learned about God from Job?

He is greater than me. He is greater than Satan. He is greater than my problems. He is under no responsibility to explain my losses to me.

10. What have we learned from Job about counseling?

Some counselors do more harm than good when they stop listening and start blaming people for their losses.

A fresh view of God due to a visit to the science center, the zoo or planetarium can help grieving people understand the greatness of God. A walk in a beautiful natural setting may help a person focus on the greatness of God.

11. What have we learned about ourselves from Job?

Being thoroughly disgusted with yourself is the first step to a personal revival. It comes by having a fresh view of the greatness of God.

Memory Verse for Chapter Three: Job 42:5-6

Chapter Four: Gideon
Discussion Questions:

1. Why do you think that the Lord chose Gideon to deliver Israel?

1 Corinthians 1:26-31 tells us that God chooses to use those who are foolish, weak, base and despised by the world to bring the glory to Himself and not to us, as it should be. Gideon was weak in the flesh, but became strong in the Spirit as we can

be. Philippians 4:13 reminds us that, "I can do all things through Christ who strengthens me."

2. How could the Lord say that Gideon was a "mighty man of valor" when Gideon hadn't won any battles?

God knows what we can be when He rules our lives. As believers we have a high position in Christ (Ephesians 1:3). Christian growth is a matter of living out the reality of who we are in Christ.

3. What is the meaning of the phrase, "the Lord is with you"?

In the Old Testament the Holy Spirit came upon people for specific tasks. Now He indwells every believer and fills those who confess known sins and yield to His will.

4. Why had God forsaken Israel to their enemies for a time?

It was a disciplinary judgment from God (Judges 6:10).

5. Why does God choose to work through people who have human weaknesses?

His strength is perfected in our weakness (2 Corinthians 12:9-10).

6. Why did Gideon need so many signs?

His faith was weak. It is good to remember that Gideon did not have the completed Bible or the great sign we have: the resurrection of Jesus Christ!

7. Why did God give Gideon so many signs?

God desires faith. Without it we cannot see His work (Hebrews 11:6).

8. Why did the Lord give Gideon a small task before sending him on the big battle?

"He who is faithful in what is least is faithful also in much" (Luke 16:10). God often tests us with small responsibilities before entrusting us with more significant tasks. Counselees should be given small homework assignments before being given big ones.

9. What have you learned from this study about God?

God is gracious in seeing us for what we can be in Christ. In the book of 1 Corinthians, Paul begins the book with high commendation of the Corinthians. Then he corrects them. Giving genuine compliments before correcting counselees lets them know that you are not trying to hurt their feelings. God understands Gideon's lack of faith and supplies the answers and the evidence he needs.

10. What have you learned from this study about counseling?

People who have a low view of themselves need to learn to see themselves in Christ (2 Corinthians 5:17). Counselees should be given doable assignments at first, and then moved on to more difficult homework assignments.

11. What have you learned from this study about yourself?

Share how you have overcome your feelings of inferiority to do what you do for the Lord.

Memory Verse for Chapter Four: Philippians 4:13

Chapter Five: Miriam
Discussion Questions:

1. Do you believe that marriage between different ethnic groups is morally wrong? Why or why not?

It is not morally wrong. The sin of intermarriage in the Old Testament related to the unequal yoking of believers and unbelievers as proved by both Rahab and Ruth being in the line of Christ according to Matthew 1:5.

2. How would you counsel a couple who wanted to marry cross-culturally?

They will have problems relating to differences in culture and possible rejection by people in both groups, but the current situation is better than it used to be.

3. Why is gossip so damaging to families and churches?

It undermines trust. Trust is the basis for loving relationships. The result is division and conflict.

4. How do you avoid gossip?

Volunteer to accompany the person as he seeks reconciliation with the offending person (Matthew 18:15-18). If they do not seek a resolution of the matter, then you should lovingly refuse to hear any more of it.

5. How do you guard the confidentiality of the counseling session?

Say, "I will do my best to keep our conversation private providing no crimes have been committed." Be aware of legal requirements for reporting abuse. Seek legal counsel and be sure to have insurance coverage for protection in lawsuits.

6. How should we respond to someone who begins sharing negative information about a Christian leader?

1 Timothy 5:19–20 "Do not receive an accusation against an elder except from two or three witnesses. [20] Those who are sinning rebuke in the presence of all, that the rest also may fear."

This passage makes it clear that Matthew 18:15-18 is to be followed in regard to leaders as well as other church members. Failure to do so is a sin.

7. How should we counsel family members who are not speaking to each other?

Bring them together if possible and seek to resolve the issues. Have them speak to you, not each other during the session. Perhaps you could begin the session by having each one write out what they think the problem is and what they have done to attempt a resolution.

8. Under what circumstances should we move from counseling to Church discipline?

If we see a person overtaken by a sinful practice that is life dominating and they reject dealing with it, then church discipline should be applied. Galatians 6:1 "Brethren, if a man is overtaken in any trespass, you who *are* spiritual restore such a one in a spirit of gentleness, considering yourself lest you also be tempted." They should be under the care of godly church leaders.

9. Can racism hinder the work of the gospel in evangelism and missions today?

God loves all people (John 3:16), so evangelism and missions is hindered by any thought of superiority or inferiority between ethnic groups.

10. What have you learned about God from this account?

God is angry when His servants are spoken against.

God can use physical illness to discipline His sinning children.

11. What have you learned about counseling from this study?

Asking questions about why people have done things can lead to solutions.

People in conflict must be brought together and assisted in resolving issues between them.

Sometimes people need "time out" to consider their actions.

12. What have you learned about yourself from this study?

Share how you have learned to properly handle problems caused by Christian leaders in a way that brings resolution and not division.

Memory Verse for Chapter 5: John 3:16

Chapter Six: David
Discussion Questions:

1. Why do men have such a problem with pornography?

Men are sexually aroused by what they see. This is why God commands men to flee immorality (1 Corinthians 6:18) as Joseph did (Genesis 39:12).

2. How would you counsel a man who is addicted to pornography?

He must remove himself from the temptation (Mark 9:43 and 47). He should then fill his mind with memorized Scriptures such as 1 John 2:15-17.

He should be encouraged to find a group of other men who are committed to holiness and meet with them for accountability and encouragement (2 Timothy 2:22).

3. How would you counsel a man who didn't work because he didn't need the money?

If a man will not work, neither should he eat (2 Thess. 3:10-12). Work was part of Adam's life before his fall into sin. God intends for us all to work for His glory in a way that helps others (Ephesians 4:28). This man should find some work that will benefit others.

4. Why did Nathan begin his counseling with a story?

David was the King. He had hidden his crimes. He wanted David to get a true sense of the gross injustice that he had committed against Uriah and most of all, God.

5. What does an outburst of anger tell you about a counselee?

There are issues in his life that are not being dealt with properly.

6. What does a lack of gratefulness have to do with immorality?

According to Romans 1:21-27, a lack of thankfulness results in vile passions such as sexual perversion.

7. What is the connection between immoral Christian leaders and the progress of evangelism and missions?

God told David that he had caused the enemy to blaspheme. God wants the nations to be glad and worship the true and living God. Immoral Christian leaders undermine the gospel message of victory over sin. But there is hope. Once David repented, he was able to teach transgressors God's ways and sinners would be converted to God (Psalm 51:13).

8. What have you learned about God in this study?

God is gracious. God is kind. God is just and holy. God disciplines His children.

9. What have you learned about counseling in this study?

We must seek God to help us lovingly reprove a proud and difficult counselee. Sometimes sinful people repent and change their ways.

10. What have you learned about yourself in this study?

Share how much easier it is for you to cover up your sins than to bring them to God and the people who can help you.

Memory Verse for Chapter 6: 1 Corinthians 6:18

Chapter Seven: Elijah
Discussion Questions:

1. Why did the Lord let Elijah sleep and then give him cake and water before the counseling session began? (verses 5-7)

Exhaustion must first be addressed physically. God made sure Elijah had rest, food and exercise before addressing his emotional and spiritual needs. Sometimes the most spiritual thing you can do is take a nap. Wise Christian counselors ask about diet, sleep and exercise when dealing with people who are "at the end of their rope".

2. Why did the Lord ask Elijah "What are you doing here?" (verse 9).

Obviously God wanted Elijah to consider the reason why he was doing what he was doing. Motives are often the real underlying issue in people's problems.

3. Why did Elijah think that he was the only one doing God's will and caring about the Lord's work? (verse 10)

He was not able to see everything so he saw the world through the "keyhole" of his own experience. He needed the larger perspective of God's view of things.

4. Why did the Lord ask Elijah again, "What are you doing here?" (verse 13)

Elijah was still in need of a new perspective.

5. Why did the Lord give him several tasks to do?

Most of us feel better when we are busy with productive work. Work was one aspect of his therapy.

6. Are you the only one who is seeking to serve the Lord in your situation?

Think about others who are serving the Lord also. Martha was busy serving but she didn't seem to realize that Mary was serving Jesus also (Luke 10:40-42).

7. What have you learned about God from this study?

God is patient with his exhausted servant and helps him work through his exhaustion to be ready to serve again.

8. What have you learned about counseling from this study?

That we should be patient with people who are sick and tired of serving others. Caregivers can become very depleted.

9. What have you learned about yourself from this study?

We should take care of ourselves with proper rest, diet and exercise so we will be able to continue to help others and serve the Lord. Share how you have learned to do this.

Memory Verse for Chapter 7: 1 Kings 19:18

Chapter Eight: Jonah
Discussion Questions:

1. Did Jonah know God well?

Yes. Jonah knew that God was gracious and merciful, slow to anger and abundant in loving-kindness, One who relents from doing harm (Jonah 4:2). He knew God, but didn't like the way He did things. He thought he could handle things better than God. Bitter people don't think that God is tough enough with their enemies.

2. How bitter was Jonah?

He was bitter enough to be depressed to the point of desiring death (Jonah 4:3).

3. Did Jonah answer God's question the first time God asked it?

No. He was apparently too bitter to think about anyone but himself and what these bad people had done to him.

4. How did God get Jonah to answer His question?

He used an object lesson of a shade plant and a worm. God has all kinds of ways to get our attention when we don't listen to Him. He can use storms, pagans, fish, plants and even worms.

5. What was God's final question to Jonah?

"Should I not pity Nineveh..?" How much do you care about people who have deeply hurt you and yours? Your ability to minister to people who have hurt you is a measure of your maturity.

6. What have you learned from this study about God?

God is kinder than we can ever be and that is why He saved sinful people like us. We should learn to love people we do not like if we are to be like God. *Matthew 5:43–48 "You have heard that it was said, 'You shall love your neighbor and hate your enemy.' ⁴⁴ But I say to you, love your enemies, bless those who curse you, do good to those who hate you, and pray for those who spitefully use you and persecute you, ⁴⁵ that you may be sons of your Father in heaven; for He makes His sun rise on the evil and on the good, and sends rain on the just and on the unjust. ⁴⁶ For if you love those who love you, what reward have you? Do not even the tax collectors do the same? ⁴⁷ And if you greet your brethren only, what do you do more than others? Do not even the tax collectors do so? ⁴⁸ Therefore you shall be perfect, just as your Father in heaven is perfect.*

7. What have you learned from this study about counseling?

We must persist in asking the probing questions that will bring counselees to face their bitterness even if they refuse to do so. We must be faithful to God.

8. What have you learned from this study about yourself?

Share how you have overcome bitterness by forgiving people who have deeply wounded your soul.

Memory Verse for Chapter 8: Matthew 5:44

Chapter Nine: Isaiah
Discussion Questions:

1. What did the death of King Uzziah have to do with the timing of the vision?

Uzziah had reigned for 52 years. His death would have created much uncertainty and insecurity for a man who cared as much as Isaiah did for this country.

2. Should worship of God cause us to evaluate ourselves?

Seeing God's holiness should cause us to consider our own sinfulness. In the New Testament, we are told to "examine ourselves" before we take communion (1 Corinthians 11:28).

3. What is the connection between counseling and worship?

Regular worship will eliminate some counseling if we can focus on Who God is and who we are on a regular basis.

4. Is there any music in Isaiah 6? What is the significance of it not being mentioned?

There is no clear mention of music in this most vital of worship passages. Music is not essential to worship. Focusing on God is vital. The Word of God is vital. Confession of sin is vital. Yielding for service is vital. Music can be a wonderful expression of worship. Singing is commanded for New Testament believers (Ephesians 5:19).

5. How can we understand the culture in which we live?

Study the conditions described in the Bible and see which ones are present in our nation today.

6. How should Christian speech be different from the general culture?

Christian speech should be truthful and gracious (John 1:17). We should never take the name of the Lord in vain (Exodus 20:7).

7. Did God tell Isaiah that he wasn't really guilty? Why not?

No, Isaiah was guilty. Guilt is real.

8. Why is our speech a good indication of our heart?

Out of the abundance of the heart the mouth speaks (Matthew 12:34).

9. Are numerical and financial successes the expected outcome of our Christian service?

Jesus said we should expect to be treated badly if we are faithful to Him. (Matthew 10:16-26).

10. Why is Isaiah 6:9-10 one of the most quoted passages in the New Testament?

Because the New Testament writers experienced the same response that God told Isaiah to expect: lack of understanding, lack of perception, heavy ears and shut eyes.

11. What have you learned from this study about God?

God is holy. God is gracious. God works through imperfect people. God's will can be accomplished through man's rebellion.

12. What have you learned in this study about counseling?

Counselees cannot serve God until they have dealt properly with their sins.

Regular worship should be part of "homework assignments".

13. What have you learned in this study about yourself?

Share how important it is to your spiritual life to worship in a good church.

Memory Verse for Chapter 9: Matthew 12:34

Chapter Ten: Daniel
Discussion Questions:

1. How did Daniel find out that the Babylonian Captivity of Israel would only last 70 years?

He read Jeremiah 25:11-12 and saw that the Babylonian Captivity was predicted by God to last only 70 years.

2. Did Daniel include himself when he confessed the sins of his nation? Why?

Yes, because as good as Daniel was, he was still a sinner (Romans 3:23).

3. Did Daniel conclude that his nation deserved the desolations of captivity? Why?

Yes. He saw the need for godly discipline (Daniel 9:13). He knew that God had a purpose in it.

4. How can we counsel our people when they become angry about what is happening to our country?

God rules over all nations (Romans 13:1). We are to submit to human government (1 Peter 2:13). We are to pray for our leaders (1 Timothy 2:1-4).

5. How important is Bible Prophecy in understanding what is going on in the world today?

The prophetic passages in Daniel, Matthew 24 and Revelation show us God's plans for the future of our world.

6. What benefits did Daniel receive personally from the counsel God gave him?

He heard that he was greatly beloved by God (Daniel 9:23). He was strengthened (Daniel 10:19).

7. What have you learned from this study about God?

God loves us (John 3:16). God has the future under His control. He has a plan for the future of Israel and the world.

8. What have you learned from this study about counseling?

Bible knowledge can help us deal with disappointments and shame for our nation.

9. What have you learned from this study about yourself?

Share how you came to understand Bible prophecy and how it has helped you face the future.

Memory Verse for Chapter 10: Daniel 9:23

Chapter Eleven: Thirsty Woman
Discussion Questions:

1. Why did Jesus need to go through Samaria? Is there some area near you that people generally avoid?

Jesus needed to go through Samaria because He loved all kinds of people. He spoke of the "good Samaritan" and prophesied that his disciples would witness concerning Him to the Samaritans in Acts 1:8.

2. Why did Jesus ask the woman at the well for a drink instead of offering to draw water for her?

By asking, He subordinated Himself to her. Asking for help places others in a superior position. Jesus took the lowest place (Philippians 2:3-11) and thus deserves the highest place.

3. Why did Jesus talk about living water? Why doesn't Jesus ever present the gospel in the same way?

Jesus often used whatever illustration was available. Jesus demonstrated that witnessing is not a canned sales talk, but a sharing of life with the dead.

4. Why did Jesus tell the woman to go and call her husband to come there?

Jesus wanted to deal with the woman at her deepest level, showing her that He alone can meet her deepest needs.

5. How did Jesus answer her question about where to worship? How would you answer someone who asked you where they should go to church?

He said that the heart of worship (spirit and truth) is a higher priority than the location of worship. In counseling, it is best to share principles of worship rather than telling people where to worship. However, as a pastor of a local church, I do not

charge money for counseling, but do require counselees to attend worship at the church I serve while I
counsel them so they can benefit from teaching that
is consistent with their counseling. Preaching and
counseling are very similar. Both are based in the
Scriptures and should involve practical application
of timeless Biblical principles.

6. What was more satisfying to Jesus than eating?

Jesus said, "My food is to do the will of Him who
sent me and to finish His work." Being used of God
to help people is more satisfying than food, just as
being saved is more satisfying than drinking water.

7. What did the disciples learn from this event?

They learned that the fields are ripe unto harvest
(John 4:35). People are ready and waiting to hear
about God's salvation in Christ. They learned that
there is joy in telling people about Jesus (John 4:36).

8. What counsel would you gain from this event that would help you counsel a person with an eating disorder?

Eating disorders can be a symptom of deeply unfulfilled needs. Every person needs Jesus. He alone can satisfy our soul's need for love, joy and peace.

9. What have you learned from this study about God?

God is humble. God is kind. God recognizes a difference between multiple marriages and living together without marriage (John 4:18). Jesus crossed religious, ethnic and gender barriers to bring salvation to lost people and so should we.

10. What have you learned from this study about counseling?

We must listen, ask probing questions, counsel people of the opposite gender in public places, avoid being sidetracked, point people to Jesus as the One who can meet their deepest needs, train other counselors, and share the joy of bringing lost people to Jesus. We should recognize that when someone is open to the gospel, someone else has gone before us to prepare the soil (John 4:38). Men should only counsel women when they are in public places. It is best if a husband and wife can counsel women together. Sometimes a wife can pick up attitudes that a husband might miss.

11. What have you learned from this study about yourself?

Share how Jesus has met the deepest needs in your life.

Memory Verse for Chapter 11: John 4:36

Chapter Twelve: The Rich Young Ruler
Discussion Questions:

1. How did Jesus define the word "good"?

God is uniquely "good". Romans 3:12 says that "there is none who does good, no not one."

Compared to God, none of us are "good". He raises the standard to a level that is impossible for man to reach without the saving work of Christ imputing His righteousness to our account (2 Corinthians 5:21).

2. Why did Jesus bring the Mosaic Law into the discussion?

He did this because the purpose of the law is to show self-righteous sinners that they cannot save themselves (1 Timothy 1:8-11).

3. How can you use the Ten Commandments in your counseling?

The Ten Commandments (Exodus 20:1-17) should be used to challenge those who don't think that they have done anything really wrong. We must help people to know they are lost before they will realize that they need to be saved (Romans 8:3).

4. What was the root problem of this young man?

It was materialistic covetousness. He was breaking the tenth commandment. That is why

Jesus told him to sell all he had and give it to the poor. Paul had the same problem according to Romans 7:7-12.

5. How would you describe the counseling techniques Jesus used with this young man?

Jesus did not jump ahead and tell the good news of the gospel to a man who was quite confident that he had already saved himself. Until this rich young ruler was convinced that he was a guilty sinner, he would have no appreciation for the gospel. Jesus loved him (Mark 10:21) enough to address him at the point of his need.

6. How did God show you that your good works did not entitle you to eternal life?

Share your testimony here of how you came to realize that you could not earn or deserve God's salvation by your good works (Ephesians 2:8-9).

7. What have you learned about God from this study?

God cares. God loves us. God deals with truth. God's law is perfect as He is. God can do that which no man can do (Mark 10:27).

8. What have you learned about counseling from this study?

Lovingly confront people with the truth. Don't move to the next step until they complete the first step. Wait for God's timing. Stop counseling if they resist obeying the truth you have shared. Encourage them to call you when they are ready to resume progress.

9. What have you learned about yourself from this study?

Share how you have had to stop working with someone in counseling when they refused to follow the clear teaching of the Bible.

Memory Verse for Chapter 12: Ephesians 2:8-9

Chapter Thirteen: The Woman Caught in Adultery
Discussion Questions:

1. Why was this woman brought to Jesus?

The religious leaders were seeking to test Jesus with difficult questions so they could trip him up and discredit him. People will test you with tricky questions that do not relate to their real problems.

2. What do you think Jesus wrote on the ground?

It could have been the Ten Commandments which God wrote on stone with His finger (Exodus 31:18). It could have been "You are weighed in the balances and found wanting" which God wrote in Daniel 5. It could have been the names of the men and the ladies they had been involved with. We don't know. Share ideas.

3. Why did Jesus get rid of this lady's accusers?

Because they were accusers with false, wicked motives who were also guilty (Romans 2:1). These hypocrites had "big beams" in their own eyes and were unfit to judge others (Matthew 7:1-5).

4. How would you deal with a person who comes to you to accuse another person?

Try to meet with both people together. Ask them both to sit down and write answers to the following questions: What is the problem? What have you done about it? How can I help? Then question each one about their answers. Require them to talk to you, the counselor, rather than to each other. Try to understand the problem by listening and observing. Open the Bible and show them how to address their difficulty.

5. Why do you think the oldest ones left first?

Perhaps because older people have lived longer and have more guilt. They also have lived long enough to see the consequences of foolish and sinful actions.

6. How should we deal with adulterers in counseling?

A clean break with the adulterous relationship must precede any attempt at reconciliation of the married couple. Confession and forgiveness are next.

7. What do you hear behind the words of Jesus: "Neither do I condemn you"?

I hear grace based on His coming sacrifice. We are already condemned because of our sins. This lady knew she was a sinner. Forgiveness is bearing the cost of another person's sin. Jesus did this on the cross. He is the great forgiver.

8. What do you see behind Jesus' counsel to "Go and sin no more"?

Holiness. Sin is destructive. Grace teaches us to live a holy life (Titus 2:12).

9. What have you learned about God from this study?

God is gracious and truthful. He is realistic about who is ready to make progress and who is not.

10. What have you learned about counseling from this study?

We must use grace and truth in counseling. We must sometimes wait for right timing.

11. What have you learned about yourself from this study?

Share your struggles to confront sinful attitudes and actions in yourself.

Memory Verse for Chapter 13: Titus 2:12

Chapter Fourteen: Thomas
Discussion Questions:

1. Why do you think Thomas failed to meet with the disciples the previous Sunday night?

People have various reasons for missing church meetings. Discuss possible scenarios of Thomas' possible confusion and grief that may have led to his skepticism.

2. Why do some people seem to lose their faith?

Exposure to intellectual superiors who are not Christians, violations of moral standards, lack of grounding can all contribute to skepticism. Discuss any other reasons why people doubt God's truths.

3. Is there a link between moral failure and skepticism?

Sometimes a violated conscience opens the door to doubts about the truth of the Bible. God's truth is intended to be held in a good conscience (1 Timothy 3:9).

4. Have you ever had doubts about the truthfulness of Christianity? How did you resolve them?

Share how you got answers to some of your questions about the inspiration of the Scriptures, the deity of Christ, the reality of Heaven, etc.

5. What evidence for Christian faith is most convincing to you?

Share what you have learned about the historical accuracy of the Bible, fulfilled prophecy, etc. Josh McDowell's "Evidence That Demands a Verdict" and "More Than a Carpenter" books are a great resource for college students writing research papers. They are also great for use in "homework assignments".

6. How are faith and worship related in your experience?

Worship without faith is an empty ritual. Worship with faith is a spiritual experience.

7. Does daily Bible reading help to strengthen your faith?

John 20:31 tells us that "these things were written that you may believe", so faith is a result of hearing God speak to us through His word by the Holy Spirit (Romans 10:17).

8. What have you learned from this study about God?

God is willing to let us examine the evidence for faith. True faith is a response to evidence. The greatest evidence is the written record of the eye-witnesses of the events recorded in the Bible.

9. What have you learned from this study about counseling?

Be patient with those who have doubts. Show them how to find answers to their questions by studying the Bible with an open heart. Pray for your counselees that God will open their eyes to the truth of the Scriptures. Honest doubts are the door to genuine faith.

10. What have you learned from this study about yourself?

Share how you have found answers to your questions about life.

Memory Verse for Chapter 14: John 20:31

Chapter Fifteen: Peter
Discussion Questions:

1. Why did Jesus wait until after breakfast to talk with Peter?

Most people are more able to respond positively after they have been fed. After a meal is a better time to have a counseling session than just before supper. Many arguments in marriage occur just before supper. A better time for dealing with difficult issues is after supper when any children are in bed.

2. Why did Jesus use his old name: Simon?

Perhaps Jesus was reminding Peter that he had not acted like "the rock" (the meaning of the name "Peter").

3. Why did Jesus remind Peter that he was Jonah's son?

Perhaps Jesus wanted Peter to think about how Jonah had been given a second chance at ministry and how God used Jonah's preaching to bring about a great Old Testament revival.

4. Why did Jesus ask Peter if he loved Jesus?

Jesus knew that Peter loved him. Perhaps he wanted Peter to remember that the greatest commandment is to love God with all our heart. Love is the greatest motive for service (Deuteronomy 6:4-6).

5. Why did Jesus ask the same basic question three times?

Peter had denied the Lord three times. Jesus wanted to open the old soul-wound and cleanse it of guilt so Peter could move on with a clear conscience.

6. What is the significance of Jesus' use of the words "lambs" and "sheep"?

The Lord wanted Peter to care for the young and the old.

7. What have you learned about God from this study?

Jesus continues to care for us even when we disappoint ourselves with our sins and weaknesses. God is gracious. He can use us in the future if we deal properly with our past.

8. What have you learned about counseling from this study?

We should follow up in prayer and initiate contact with the people who have hurt and separated from us. The most difficult people to help are our critics. "Feeding the hand that bites you" is one of the greatest challenges in ministry.

9. What have you learned about yourself from this study?

Share how the Lord has been willing to use you in spite of your failures and sins. God can make a "straight lick with a crooked stick" but only after the person has confessed the sin and returned to fellowship with the Lord by yielding to His leadership by His Spirit through the Word of God, the Bible.

Memory Verse for Chapter 15: Deuteronomy 6:5

Chapter Sixteen: Paul
Discussion Questions:

1. What do you think Paul's thorn was?

We don't know. Some think it was an eye problem because of Galatians 6:11 and Galatians 4:13-15.

2. How does Satan buffet Christians today?

He uses temptations, trials, illness, family problems, losses, etc.

3. How should you pray about your thorns?

Ask God for their removal or grace to bear them; whatever is best in His will for you.

4. How would you counsel someone who thought he was oppressed by demons?

Go to Ephesians 6:10-20 and explain spiritual warfare. Deal with sin and salvation. When Jesus comes into a life, the demons go out. The armor of God is used in prayer. "Greater is He that is in you than he who is in the world" (1 John 4:4).

5. How is God's grace sufficient for your "thorns"?

Share how God has given you grace to bear a "thorn" in your life. Share how He has enabled you to continue to serve Him, your family and others in spite of "thorns".

6. What infirmities has God used in your life?

Share the benefits of having a "thorn": humility, opportunities to minister, etc.

7. How determined are you to finish well?

Share how you want to hear the Lord say, "Well done, you good and faithful servant" (Matthew 25:23).

8. What have you learned about God from this study?

God is in control of all things: the Devil, disease, people, and the world. He sometimes chooses to say "No!" to His children when He wants to develop some grace in our lives.

9. What have you learned about counseling from this study?

People need to know that God is in control. He cares and He will give us grace to bear our trials if we seek Him in trusting prayer (1 John 5:14-15).

10. What have you learned about yourself from this study?

Share how you have learned that you should not give up when you fail the Lord. He loves you and is willing to use anyone who has a humble and submissive heart.

Memory Verse for Chapter 16: 2 Corinthians 12:9

SUMMARY OF COUNSELING TECHNIQUES OF THE "WONDERFUL COUNSELOR":

1. He asked many questions even though He already knew all the answers. He wanted His counselees to think about their motives and their actions.

2. He gave them choices and explained the outcome of those choices. This demonstrates His respect for human authority under divine sovereignty.

3. He showed patience, grace and truth in all He said to people with problems.

4. He gave wise insights into the nature of reality so as to inform decisions.

5. He showed interest in justice as well as mercy. He cared deeply about injustice.

6. He listened well and adjusted assignments when the counselee complained.

7. He showed respect for imperfect human authority figures and encouraged people to function within their roles.

8. He understood that some children will be more "wild"' than others, but all people need the Lord.

9. He saw opportunities that His counselees did not see and helped them discover them for themselves.

10. He showed his counselees His greatness as demonstrated in His creation. He revealed their dependence on God.

11. He worked through people and linked counselees with others who could help them through prayer.

12. He worked to reconcile broken relationships between counselees and their loved ones.

13. He called meetings with people in conflict and helped them to resolve issues by listening, speaking truth and rendering judgments.

14. He "backed up" His servants when they were unjustly criticized.

15. He used a "time out" to give a counselee time to process her discipline and be sorry and repentant.

16. He backed up His counsel with discipline. Today, Christian counselors should back up their Biblical counsel with church discipline.

17. He sought to bring counselees to a place of repentance for their sins so there would be hope of mercy.

18. He recognized the importance of addressing the physical, emotional and spiritual aspects of people's problems.

19. He knew exactly what each person's deepest need was ... they needed Him.

20. He did not attempt to help people who refused to agree with His diagnosis.

21. He confronted people who had a critical spirit of false accusation.

22. He counseled individual women in public places.

23. He did not move to the next step with a counselee until they had completed the assigned task.

God is the Wonderful Counselor!

CONCLUSION:

I was teaching a class in Vacation Bible School. Our theme was the Jewish Temple and I was playing the part of the high priest in the drama. After the class, we had our refreshment break. I was drinking Koolaid and cookies in my high priest outfit when a very small boy approached me very confidently. "I know who you are!" he exclaimed, "You're God!" (He had apparently missed the point of our lesson and had jumped to his own conclusions.) I bent down very low and looked him in the eye. I said, "There are two things I am sure of, young man, there is a God and I'm not Him." I don't know if he got it or not, but I wonder about you. Have you learned those two great facts? There is a God and you are not Him. When it comes to counseling people with problems, I have learned that I am not the answer to anyone's problem. But I do know the One Who is the answer to the biggest problem that we all have. Our biggest problem is that we are sinners and make a mess of our lives when we do things our way. When we listen to the "Wonderful Counselor", we have wisdom. James 1:5 says that if we lack wisdom, we should ask God for it and He will give it to us. That is a promise of God. Ask God in faith for the wisdom you need today and He will give it to you through the Name of Jesus Christ and the power of the Holy Spirit in the Word of God, the Bible.

ABOUT THE AUTHOR:

Dan Peters is Senior Pastor of Limerick Chapel where he has served for 25 years. He has been a pastor for 43 years, serving churches in Pennsylvania and Maryland. His lovely wife, Diane, and Dan have been blessed with six children, all grown, and nine grandchildren. Dan studied at Cairn University (B.S in Bible), Biblical Seminary and Berean Graduate School of Theology (D. Min.) He studied Biblical Counseling under Dr. Jay Adams and Dr. John Bettler at the Christian Counseling and Educational Foundation while a student at Biblical Seminary. Dan enjoys preaching, counseling, studying, reading, walking, riding his cruiser and yard work. His radio ministry is on WFIL in Philadelphia and on WBYN in Boyertown, PA. Dan is available to speak at seminars and conferences on this and other subjects for churches, pastors' fellowships, mission workers, colleges and seminaries.

CPSIA information can be obtained at www.ICGtesting.com
Printed in the USA
BVOW04s2108061214

378058BV00003B/9/P